Photo Album
Quilts

Photo Album
Quilts

Wendy Butler Berns

LARK BOOKS
A Division of Sterling Publishing Co., Inc.
New York / London

A Red Lips 4 Courage Communications, Inc. book

www.redlips4courage.com

Eileen Cannon Paulin
President

Catherine Risling
Director of Editorial

Editor
Erika Kotite

Photographer
Zachary Williams
Williams Visual

Copy Editors
Catherine Risling
Darra Williamson

Photo Stylist
Catherine Risling

Book Designers
Jocelyn Foye
Rose Sheifer-Wright

Dedication

To my family, who has been so supportive
to the crazy quilter in the house.

Library of Congress, Cataloging-in-Publication Data

Berns, Wendy Butler.

Photo album quilts / Wendy Butler Berns.

     p. cm.

  Includes index.

  ISBN-13: 978-1-60059-189-1

  ISBN-10: 1-60059-189-2

  1. Patchwork. 2. Photographs on cloth. I. Title.

TT835.B3567 2007

746.46'041--dc22

                       2007019944

10 9 8 7 6 5 4 3 2 1

First Edition

Published by Lark Books, A Division of Sterling Publishing Co., Inc.
387 Park Avenue South, New York, NY 10016

Distributed in Canada by Sterling Publishing, c/o Canadian Manda
Group, 165 Dufferin Street Toronto, Ontario, Canada M6K 3H6

Distributed in the United Kingdom by GMC Distribution Services,
Castle Place, 166 High Street, Lewes, East Sussex, England BN7 1XU

Distributed in Australia by Capricorn Link (Australia) Pty Ltd.,
P.O. Box 704, Windsor, NSW 2756 Australia

If you have questions or comments about this book, please contact:
Lark Books, 67 Broadway, Asheville, NC 28801, (828) 253-0467

Manufactured in China
All rights reserved
ISBN 13: 978-1-60059-189-1
ISBN 10: 1-60059-189-2

For information about custom editions, special sales, premium and
corporate purchases, please contact Sterling Special Sales
Department at (800) 805-5489; or e-mail specialsales@sterlingpub.com.

Table of Contents

Foreword

There are many talented quilters, all very dedicated to their work. Some create quilts in the classic style so that their quilts can be used in everyday life. This has been the tradition of quilts throughout history and it continues today.

Then there are the quilters who want their work to be held to a different standard. They have pushed beyond the traditional boundaries of the quilt to create a true piece of art. These quilters use original designs and ideas to convey their feelings and emotions in their work. They want to tell stories and celebrate life with their quilts. Wendy Butler Berns is such a storyteller.

Wendy's love for her family and a passionate and knowledgeable interest in the flora and fauna that surrounds us is a strong theme that permeates her work. Her meticulous ability to capture a moment in time is uncanny. Translating these gems of time into fabric is done with the utmost skill and craftsmanship.

As the pages of this wonderful book unfold, so will the special talent and insight of an artist who knows the secret of expressing everyday life in her quilts. Enjoy the journey and be prepared to share in Wendy's creative response to making quilts that share a familiar life story.

—Denise Tallon Havlan
Award-winning fiber artist

CHAPTER ONE

Getting Started

You can learn these concepts and then adapt them to suit your own designs.

Every quilting process needs a special technique so that the creator can better define his or her own unique art. In this and the following chapters, I introduce the basic components of my picture-image appliqué technique, which I've developed over years of much trial (and just a bit of error). These steps have proven successful over and over and I am delighted every time another memory is preserved in a new quilt.

In addition to providing you suggestions for the set-up and supplies you need, this chapter offers some insights into choosing your photo, adapting it to a line drawing, and then selecting the fabrics that will make it come to life. The ultimate goal is for you to master the technique with little guesswork.

A Comfortable Workspace

You can adapt any nook or cranny available to create a comfortable workspace. In the early steps of the process, you will need adequate table space to prepare your glue stick and freezer paper templates. You will want to have an ironing board nearby. A secretary chair is great for swiveling between the table and ironing board.

When the quilt design is large, work in sections on the table, and then move to a larger hard surface to glue appliqué the sections together. Your cutting table, a large kitchen counter island, or—in a pinch—an uncarpeted bedroom, living room, or kitchen floor will work.

Creating a Design Wall

A design wall is an effective way to view your project from a distance. A design wall can be as simple as a flannel-backed tablecloth taped to a wall. For a more permanent setup, purchase two 4' x 8' insulation boards from your local hardware store, cover them with gray flannel or felt, and bolt the boards to the wall.

Storing Your Fabric

Sort your fabrics by value—that is, from lightest to darkest—within the colors of the color wheel (learn more about the color wheel in the following Tools section). This will help you access fabrics easily when it is time to choose them for your project. Stack the sorted fabrics in clear drawers by color or, better yet, stack them on shelves in an old cupboard or armoire with doors that you can close to protect the fabrics from light.

Tools

The following pages describe what you need to build your photo album quilts. Many of these tools are very basic, and can be found at quilt and craft stores.

Adhesives

You need cellophane tape for attaching newsprint to the wall, attaching copy paper to transparency film, and

attaching fabric swatches to pattern pieces; washable, permanent white glue sticks for adhering your freezer paper/ fabric pattern pieces to each other; and masking tape for attaching two pieces of freezer paper together when preparing to trace your Master Image Map.

Color Wheel

There are 12 pure colors used in pigments and dyes. Starting with the three primary colors (red, yellow, and blue), a color wheel shows their corresponding secondary and tertiary colors in relationship order.

Use a color wheel to help sort your fabrics by the 12 color segments and then within each segment, sort by value from light to dark. All the colors on the color wheel relate to each other in some fashion. Use it to choose color combinations for a future project.

If you choose only one color such as red, that is a monochromatic color scheme. To make this choice successful though, you need to have a wide array of red in many values for impact.

Direct complements are across from each other on the wheel, such as red and green or yellow and purple. An analogous color combination is a group of colors next to each other such as red, red orange, orange, and yellow-orange; these would be a great combination for a quilt with an autumn feel.

A triad is when you choose three colors equidistant to each other. The color combinations of red, yellow, and blue or green, violet, and orange are both triads.

Iron and Ironing Board

You will need a standard household iron with a steam setting for adhering freezer paper to fabric and for pressing fabric seams.

Light Box

Light boxes come in several sizes and are sold at photograph and/or art supply stores.

These boxes are useful for tracing original photographs and evaluating your fabric choices when the fabrics are covered by freezer paper. If you do not have a light box, a light-filled window will do the trick.

Color wheel with 12 color segments, including pure hues, tints, and shades.

Overhead Projector

An overhead projector is useful for enlarging your design to create the Master Image Map. Don't go out and buy a projector if you are just beginning to quilt; a copy center can easily enlarge your design for you.

Reducing Glass

A reducing glass is a little door peephole sold at hardware stores. This tool allows you to view the effectiveness of your fabric choices and overall design from a distance. As an alternative, you can view your design from the wrong end of a pair of binoculars.

Rotary Cutter, Mat, and Ruler

These handy tools, which can be found wherever quilting supplies are sold, help you make even, straight cuts as you prepare your fabric, cut larger pieces into strips, and trim your quilts for finishing. Mats range in size and are used to protect your tabletop surface. The rotary cutter looks a bit like a pizza cutter with its round, razor-sharp blade. Rulers come in many different types and sizes; 6" x 24" is a good, versatile size to have on hand for these quilts.

Scissors

You need two pairs of scissors: one for paper and another pair of sharp, good-quality fabric scissors with 3"–5" blades. Also, small scissors are great for clipping threads.

Sewing Machine and Accessories

Your sewing machine should be in good working order and have a zigzag, a darning/free-motion, and a walking foot. You will use the zigzag and free-motion feet for quilting and appliqué, and the walking foot for quilting and attaching bindings. Keep a supply of sharp 80/12 sewing machine needles on hand.

Stiletto or Seam Ripper

You will want a sharp tool such as a stiletto, the edge of a seam ripper, or even a small nail or wooden toothpick to turn under seams and to gently remove unwanted freezer paper/fabric pattern pieces if they are not working in your design.

Supplies

Each quilt may vary a bit in terms of the number of fabrics you will use; but they all will require the same basic list of supplies. To create a project approximately 18" x 24", you will need the following:

A. Photo: original enlarged to 8" x 10"
B. Stiletto
C. Adhesive tape: cellophane and masking
D. Sewing needles
E. Pins: ½" straight and safety (50–100)
F. Threads: monofilament, clear and smoke; cottons, polyester, rayons, assorted
G. Markers: extra/ultra-fine permanent black, blue, green, red
H. Scissors: fabric and paper
I. Fabric: 100 percent cotton
J. Fine-line, blue, water-soluble pen
K. Sharp pencils and eraser
L. Glue sticks
M. Copy paper: 4–6 sheets

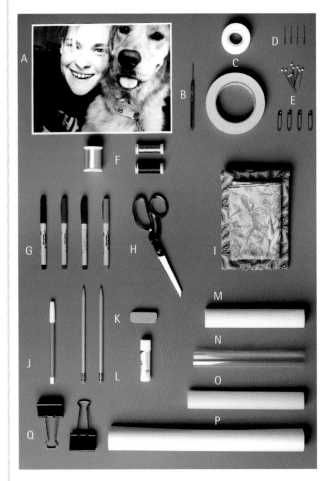

N. Tracing paper or transparency film: 4–6 pieces
O. Freezer paper: 2 yards (15"–18" wide)
P. Fusible stabilizer: 1 yard (42" wide)
Q. Binder clips: large, heavy duty (8–12)

Use What You Have

I challenge myself to make do with the fabrics I have and, in the beginning, I suggest you do the same. As you gain experience with each quilt, and work with your fabrics more, you can add to your stash in a more informed manner, and build a broader selection of special prints or a wider range of values.

Techniques

The appliqué process used to create a photo album quilt involves translating an image from a line drawing into a paper pattern, and then choosing fabrics to best interpret the image. The fabric pieces cut with the freezer paper pattern template pieces are temporarily bonded together with a glue stick. Then all of them are appliquéd in place using an invisible free-motion zigzag stitch. Finally, the project is layered and quilted.

Choosing Photos

When it's time to begin your quilt project, sort through a variety of photographs that you love. If you choose a human figure as the subject matter, consider using a photo with a profile shot, or one where the figure is turned partially away from the camera. A full-view face is tricky to recreate, so I suggest waiting until you have more experience before tackling this type of image. When you are ready for this challenge, refer to Chapter 3 for tips on capturing the human face.

Photos that evoke some kind of emotion are very appealing to work with—a figure quietly staring into the distance, a puppy licking the nose of a child, the look of concentration on a cyclist's face. This emotion will have added appeal for you, the quilter, as well as for the viewer of the quilt; it connects you more closely to the subject matter, which will help motivate you and keep your interest focused.

If you are new to the picture-image appliqué process, I suggest choosing a photo with a simple composition. View your first few small quilts as thumbnail sketches to prepare you for making more complex quilts later. To start, select an image with a single figure, or trace only one figure from the photo. Consider cropping the figure to include just the head and shoulders.

Once you have decided on the image, crop the photo to that simple composition, then enlarge the photo, in either color or black and white, to approximately 8" x 10". Your goal is to obtain as crisp an image as possible for tracing. Cropping and enlarging your photo can be done on a copy machine or by using a photo-editing program on your computer. Here are some examples of photographs and the simplified line drawings I made from them.

Original photo

Line drawing

Original photo

Line drawing

Original photo

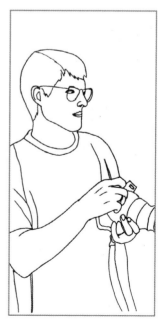
Line drawing

Creating a Simple Line Drawing

The smaller the quilt, the simpler the line drawing must be so that when the drawing is finalized and enlarged, the templates will be a reasonable size to work with. When you decide you are ready to use the full body of your subject, consider a quilt size about 40" x 40".

You can trace your photo in one of two ways. The first option is to use tracing paper, a pencil, and a permanent marker. Place the enlarged photograph on a light box or tape the enlargement to a light-filled window. Next, tape the tracing paper over the image and use a sharp pencil to make your tracings. Once you are satisfied, mark over the pencil lines with an ultra-fine black permanent marker. Finally, use a large eraser to remove any visible pencil lines.

The second method is to use transparency film and an ultra-fine black permanent marker. The transparency film is very clear and easy to see through, so you can work directly at your table. Tape the photo to desired surface, tape the transparency film over the photo, and then complete your tracing lines with the black marker. Work carefully; since the marker is permanent, you cannot erase a line if you want to make a change.

Whether you use tracing paper or transparency film, begin by outlining the figure, clothing, and hair, and then draw a few lines for folds in the fabric or to denote shadow. For the background, trace only a few lines here and there for reference.

Check your progress occasionally by slipping a piece of plain white copy paper between your enlargement and the traced outline so you can see how precise your lines are.

Perfect Lines

Obtaining a crisp line drawing is a crucial first step to a successful quilt. It is worth experimenting with several drafts to obtain a line drawing that satisfies you. At this stage, there is no exact right or wrong result. Trust your eyes to decide what you like best.

As you trace your photograph either on tracing paper or transparency film, use a piece of plain paper to check your line drawing as you go.

Enlarging the Final Drawing

When you are satisfied with the line drawing, it is time to enlarge it to the full size of your quilt. This can be done at a copy center or with an overhead projector.

Copy Center Method: The simplest method for enlarging your line drawing is to take it to a copy or blueprint center. This is a little pricey, but choosing this method means the line drawing will come out exactly as you drew it.

Tape the line drawing you created on tracing paper or transparency film to a piece of white copy paper so the tracing lines show clearly.

Decide the final size of your quilt. For your first several projects—for example, where you have cropped your subject—start small (between 18" and 24"). When you have several quilts completed, tackle the full body of your subject, and target the finished quilt to finish between approximately 30" x 40" and 40" x 40".

At the copy center, use a proportion scale to determine what percentage you need to make your enlargement. For example, if the original line drawing is 8" x 10" and you want to enlarge it to 18" x 24", you will need to enlarge the original approximately 225 percent. Many larger copy centers have machines with paper that measures up to 36" wide; this allows you to enlarge your drawing in increments up to 400 percent.

Overhead Projector Method: If you have access to an overhead projector, use transparency film and a fine permanent marker for tracing. Once you have traced your line drawing onto the transparency film, place the film on the projector and move the projector back from the wall until the image reaches the desired size. Tape a large sheet of newsprint to the wall and trace the enlarged outline onto it to create a pattern.

Creating the Master Image Map and Templates

Once your line drawing is enlarged to the full size of the quilt you want to create, you will be able to see the open areas of the design more easily. You will also be able to determine how you should segment those spaces into workable templates for your Master Image Map.

To do this, ask yourself these questions:
- Do I want to create a sense of movement with curved lines, or do I prefer a more linear feel with more straight lines?
- How many sections do I want for the hair?
- What is the best way to segment the clothing to keep the lines simple, but at the same time create a sense of dimension and depth?
- Do I want to use a special piece of fabric to create a whole-cloth background, or do I want to segment the background to create additional interest?

You will label each piece and add tic marks/registration marks when you trace the design lines onto the dull side of freezer paper. Then you will cut the freezer paper apart to make working templates. More details on this step are covered in Chapter 2.

Important: The segmented line drawing will become your Master Image Map. It serves as a road map and should never be cut apart.

Curved lines take a little more effort to assemble, but they will give your finished piece a wonderful sense of movement and flow.

Straight lines on the template pieces are easier to assemble. They can be used as a design element and will give your finished piece a more static feel.

Here is an example for segmenting hair using larger segments. Follow the rounded lines of the head as a guide.

Try more intricate lines for added detail as you segment hair.

Choosing the Fabrics

Finally the fabrics! My absolute *favorite* part of quilting is selecting the fabrics for my quilts. I love combining many different types of prints to create the mood or texture I visualize for the quilt design.

I primarily use quilter's cottons, occasionally adding a cotton velveteen or sparkly specialty fabric for extra texture or visual depth. It is fun to include prints of various scale (small, medium, and large), geometrics, stripes, and fabrics with a mottled, dappled, or other unique visual texture. I consider value very carefully to be sure that there is enough contrast between the various design elements. The drama in quilt design is created with a broad range of values.

When choosing fabrics for my photo album quilts, I look at my fabrics differently than if I were choosing them for a traditional patchwork quilt. Suddenly I see skin tones, swirling hair, textured mountains, garden undergrowth, or flower centers. In all my quilts, I use three to four fabrics in my segmented areas where another quilter might use only one. I like to evoke visual excitement for the viewer, so I work mostly with prints and use relatively few solids.

More fabric gives you more options; however, you do not need large quantities of any one fabric. I have lots of fat quarters (cuts of fabrics that measure 18" x 22") and ½-yard cuts of many values within my fabric stash. Your own stash will begin to resemble Swiss cheese after you have cut many pieces from it.

To audition fabrics for different sections of your quilt, fan prospective fabrics by value, and step back to view them from a distance. You want to be conscious of the value of each fabric so that the design elements within your quilt contrast with each other. When you choose multiple fabrics of similar value (*e.g.* for hair), you'll want to make sure they transition more smoothly.

Use binoculars or a reducing glass, or simply squint at your choices to study how the fabrics relate to each other. When I am auditioning potential fabrics, my studio floor looks like a tornado passed through. Prospective fabrics are everywhere. I love the process of exploring the different options.

While you will want to play and experiment for a while, eventually it is time to move on. Narrow down your choices and begin to determine where each fabric will go.

Fabrics depicting skin tones.

Fabrics depicting swirling hair.

Fabrics depicting textured mountains.

Fabrics depicting garden undergrowth.

A head of hair is created using three to five fabrics of the same value.

For more visual excitement I tend to choose fabrics with mottled combinations of design and color.

Some Final Words of Wisdom

Choosing fabrics can be an anxious process for many. Again, trust your instincts and give yourself permission to jump in and take a chance. Each choice is a learning process and you can always revise a choice later. Part of the artistic process is to experiment and see what happens.

I know that my quilts will always be an interpretation of my photo. I choose to make each one an impressionistic interpretation rather than try to duplicate the photo exactly. This thought process reduces my anxiety and allows me to move forward.

As soon as the line drawing is transformed into fabric, the piece takes on a whole life of its own.

The Flip Side

Occasionally, the back of a fabric may be just the value you are looking for. Take a peek on the back to see.

CHAPTER TWO

The Step-by-Step Process

It all starts with a master pattern, which will serve as your trusty guide for pulling all of the colors and pieces of your quilt together.

Once you've chosen the subject and basic design for your photo image appliqué, it's time to understand the quilt-making procedures from beginning to end. This chapter provides an overview of the complete step-by-step process for creating a photo album quilt.

For me, it is helpful to see the "road map" as I begin, so I understand the whole picture and know where I am headed. With an array of visual examples to assist you, I will touch on creating your master pattern, making freezer paper templates, how to use my glue stick appliqué and machine appliqué techniques, and finally, some highlights of the finishing touches that will make your quilt extraordinary.

After enlarging your paper pattern (this one is 45" x 45"), place the segmenting lines on what is now the Master Image Map.

Master Image Map

The first step to make a photo album quilt is preparing the map from which you will create all of your template pieces. Start by enlarging your original paper pattern line drawing to the desired finished size of your quilt.

Then subdivide the enlarged paper pattern into sections. Label all pieces by number or letter in a system that makes sense to you; for example, hair—H1, H2, H3, H4; shirt—S1, S2, S3, S4, and so on (Fig. 1).

This original copy, with all its labeled and marked pattern pieces, is your Master Image Map, and you will use it to determine how to reassemble your template pieces. Do not cut the map apart—it is like the picture on the box of a jigsaw puzzle, and you will refer to it again and again.

Fig. 1

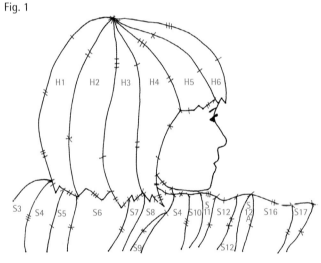

Preparing Your Fabrics

Whenever possible, launder the cotton and other washable fabrics you plan to use. The finish on some fabrics prevents the glue from adhering properly for the appliqué process. In particular, unwashed batik fabrics have more difficulty holding the glue. This may be due to the surplus wax left in the fabric following the batiking process.

Preparing Freezer Paper Templates

Cut a piece of freezer paper to measure 1½" larger than your Master Image Map on all sides. If freezer paper is not wide enough, piece required number of sheets together shiny side down, overlapping edges by about ½", and joining each sheet with a single strip of masking tape. (Masking tape will not melt when pressed.) Center freezer paper shiny side down over your Master Image Map, taping corners of both to hold them securely.

Use an extra-fine black permanent marker to trace all lines of the Master Image Map onto the dull side of the freezer paper. Label all pieces and transfer tic marks (see Fig. 2) and the lettering or numbering codes you have chosen for all pieces.

Use extra-fine blue or green permanent markers to place tic marks along seam lines, using marks such as I, II, III, IV, V, and so on (Fig. 2). These marks should intersect seam lines so they will appear on both sides of template pattern pieces when pieces are cut apart. Place a tic mark about every 3", and make a red slash at each seam junction.

Fig. 2

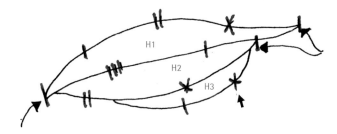

Cutting and Using Templates

Carefully cut apart paper template pieces, cutting along black traced lines as exactly as possible. Work one section at a time to avoid confusing pattern pieces; for example, cut hair templates first.

When you are finished cutting one section of templates, take the pieces to the ironing board. Use a hot steam iron to press freezer paper templates shiny side down to *front* of the appropriate fabric, allowing an approximate ¼" seam allowance all around. Hold iron in place for three to five seconds. Some fabrics may need a few more seconds.

Cut fabric around each template, adding a ¼" seam allowance (Fig. 3). A wider seam will be difficult to turn under. Clip fabric every ½" to 1" around concave and convex curves for easier turning.

Fig. 3

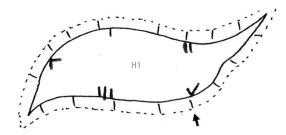

Assembling Template Pieces

Cover your worktable to protect it from glue stick smears. Line template pieces on your worktable in order you plan to glue them. Then, choose between two types of edges for your appliqué.

Finished edge: For a turned-under, finished edge, glue template pieces in sequence (Fig. 4). In the following example, you would work as follows:

1. Glue H1 seam allowance A under, flush with edge of freezer paper.

2. Swipe glue stick along seam allowance B of piece H2, and then snuggle H1 next to H2, aligning tic marks. Keep glued sections as flat as possible as you work to allow glue to set.

3. Continue to work in sections. As each section is completed, adhere individual sections together using glue stick until the whole project top is completed.

Fig. 4

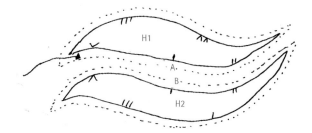

Trimming Seams with Ease

For intricate areas such as around the nose, mouth, and fingers, it is helpful to trim seams down to ⅛" and clip closely before turning and gluing (Fig. 1). Remember that using a sharp, pointed tool such as a stiletto, wooden toothpick, or tip of a seam ripper will help in turning these more intricate edges (Fig. 2).

Fig. 1   Fig. 2

Take a Peek

You will get to a point where all fabric is hidden behind freezer paper templates. Here are two methods for sneaking a peek.

- Remove a few freezer paper templates to check the fabrics, and then iron the templates back in place. (The freezer paper will adhere three or four times before the glue wears out.) The tic marks on the pattern pieces will help you place your next pieces in their proper positions.

- Carefully hold a section of glued templates up to a light source—either a window or a bright lamp. The fabric will show through the freezer paper well enough to give you a sense of how the fabrics are blending and contrasting with each other.

Fig. 5

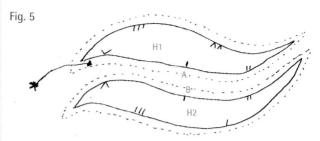

Raw edge: For a more textured look, you may prefer portions of the appliqué to have raw edges (Fig. 5). Examples might be when you want the edges of hair to be wispier, or the edges of a flower to have a softer finish.

1. Trim seam allowance A of H1 flush with freezer paper.

2. Swipe glue stick along seam allowance B of piece H2, and then snuggle H1 raw edge next to H2. Keep glued sections as flat as possible as you work to allow glue to set.

3. Continue to work in sections. As each section is completed, adhere individual sections together using glue stick until the whole project top is completed.

This coneflower in *Little Gardener II* is created with turned-under edges.

Removing Templates

Allow glue to set up briefly before carefully removing freezer paper. If necessary, use a sharp tool such as a stiletto, nail, wooden toothpick, or end of a seam ripper to slip under the freezer paper when peeling it off the fabric. Glued seams will be a bit fragile; if glue does not hold the seam completely, simply reapply a bit of glue to adhere seams back together.

Place glued project on the design wall and stand back to evaluate your fabric choices. View your project using a reducing glass or other similar tool. Be sure contrast between different elements is strong enough so that the design is visible and pleasing. When you are using fabrics of similar value, such as for hair, be sure fabrics make a smooth transition from one to another.

If one or more fabrics are not working visually, gently remove that template piece with a sharp tool such as a stiletto or toothpick, carefully running point of tool between glued seams to ease them apart. Use that template pattern piece to cut a new piece from different fabric, and then slide and glue new fabric choice back in place.

Reinforcing the Design

Since, at this point, all seams are only glued, your project is very fragile. I have found a technique that works well to hold my pieces in place until I am ready to begin machine appliquéing and embellishing: I fuse the delicate project to a fusible stabilizer. This process reinforces the piece while I machine appliqué, or do any decorative machine embellishing I might choose.

Adding stabilizer to your project creates a fourth layer in your quilt. Some traditional quilters may be uncomfortable including this fourth layer, but actually the extra layer is quite effective for a wall quilt. The stabilizer softens with handling and adds a bit more weight and support, helping the quilt hang better.

Supplies
- Fusible stabilizer
- Iron and ironing surface
- Straight pins

Instructions

1. Cut fusible stabilizer about ¼" smaller than project to prevent hot iron from coming in contact with it. Place fusible stabilizer shiny side *up* on the *back* of the glue-appliquéd project. Pin glued quilt top to stabilizer and attach to your design wall. Take one more look from a distance to be sure you are satisfied with fabrics.

2. Working from center of project to outer edges, use a hot iron and steam to fuse stabilizer to project, with slow, tapping strokes. Stabilizer fuses much more slowly than fusible web, so you may need to hold iron in place for 8 to 10 seconds before moving to a new area. By working from center out, you will prevent wrinkles and puckers from forming on both stabilizer and glue-appliquéd top.

The Big Picture: Evaluating a Large Project

To secure a larger project for viewing on the design wall, all you need is some fusible stabilizer and straight pins. To do:

1. Cut fusible stabilizer ¼" smaller than size of the project. Slide stabilizer under your glued appliqué, and then secure project to stabilizer using many straight pins. This holds fragile glued seams together.

2. Pin project to design wall and step back to look *carefully* at how fabrics are working together. This extra step allows you to confirm your fabric choices and to catch anything that is not working.

3. When you are satisfied with your design, fuse the stabilizer to the project.

Some Thoughts on Thread

There are several brands of monofilament threads on the market. These threads have numerous uses in quilting and come in either polyester or nylon. Use clear thread on lighter colored fabrics and smoke-colored thread on darker fabrics. Purchase good-quality thread for the best success.

As you change thread colors in the top of your machine, polyester or nylon monofilament in the bobbin does not peek through to the surface of your quilt as another neutral-colored thread might. The thread works successfully when paired with most cotton, rayon, and polyester threads of standard weight. The success rate is reduced with metallic or other heavier-weight threads.

Using polyester or nylon monofilament thread in the bobbin also reduces the amount of adjustment you need to make in your thread tension, but some sewing machines may be fussy about using it there. This thread has a lot of give and has a tendency to stretch. When winding it on a bobbin, wind as slowly as possible and take care not to fill the bobbin completely. When the bobbin is wound too quickly, the thread stretches; it relaxes to its original state when you stitch with it, causing puckering or poor tension for the top thread.

Finally, monofilament thread may warp a plastic bobbin, so experiment with it to see if it works successfully with your machine.

Machine Appliqué

Prepare your sewing machine with clear or smoke-colored polyester or nylon monofilament thread on top and a neutral-colored thread or monofilament in the bobbin. Use either a darning foot with a free-motion zigzag foot or a regular zigzag foot with the feed dogs engaged.

Darning/Free-Motion Foot

I like using a darning foot and a tiny, free-motion zigzag stitch width (1.5) to free-motion appliqué along each glue-appliquéd seam. Make up a sample and test the zigzag width on your machine to be certain it gives the look you want, and then stitch all the glued seams in place. Use a slightly wider zigzag stitch (about 2.0) for raw edges.

Regular Zigzag Foot

If you are not comfortable with free-motion stitching, keep the feed dogs engaged, and use a regular zigzag foot or darning with the same tiny stitch width (1.5) to stitch all glued seams in place. (Adjust the stitch width to 2.0 for raw edges.)

To secure starting and finishing stitches with a regular zigzag foot or darning foot, backstitch several stitches each time you start and finish a seam.

Machine Embellishing

I love adding extra dimension and texture to my quilts by incorporating many of the specialty threads, yarns, and fibers available. I prefer to do this embellishing on a quilt top that has been stabilized with fusible stabilizer before layering and quilting.

Simple machine stitching with thread allows me to enhance facial features such as eyelashes, beards, or mustaches. Extra doodling or thread painting on tree trunks or around flower petals or leaves creates a more pronounced line. This is particularly effective when I have used the raw-edge appliqué method.

Using yarn couched in place with monofilament thread and a small zigzag stitch allows me to create unique flower stems, a climbing rope, or a textured inner border.

Machine Embellishment Examples

The tiny pine tree and its fine needles in *The Bear and the Boy—I Spy the Disappearing Bear's Paw* were created with various green and brown threads and embellishing stitches.

Embellishing stitches around the daffodil's petals and along the stem in *Remembering...in the Spring* adds dimension to the yellow flower.

In *Little Gardener I,* flower stems were created by twisting two different textured yarns together and couching them in place with monofilament thread and a tiny zigzag stitch.

For George's beard in *George the Entomologist—Catches the Quilting Bug*, I chose a printed white fabric for the template piece. Using white rayon thread, I doodled with long scribbling stitches to create the whiskers.

Couching

Couching lets you add dimensional pieces to your quilt top by attaching a thick thread or yarn with a zigzag stitch. All kinds of yarn, string, and ribbon can be used in various ways. For example, you might want to add texture to a tree trunk, outline an image for added emphasis, create flower stems, or add texture to an inner border of a quilt. The ideas are endless.

To prepare for couching, set your machine at a zigzag stitch the width of the yarn you plan to use. Couching can be done with a regular zigzag foot or a darning/free-motion foot. I prefer to use a polyester or nylon monofilament thread in clear or smoke so it will blend into the fibers of the yarn.

In the spot you plan to attach the couched yarn, leave a tiny section of the appliqué unstitched so you can tuck your yarn ends underneath.

Vary the color and thickness of the stems by twisting several different strands of yarn together. Position the yarn when the machine appliqué is completed, leaving a tiny

Fig. 6 Fig. 7

A single strand of yarn can be used as you couch. For more dimension, twist several strands of yarn together (Fig. 6). Set the zigzag stitch so that the couching stitches are the width of the twisted yarn (Fig. 7). Secure the ends of the yarn in place either by zigzagging back and forth for a few stitches, or tucking yarn under design elements such as a flower, and couch in place.

section of the stem unstitched to tuck under at the open spot in the appliqué. Thread the machine with polyester or nylon monofilament thread, and set the zigzag stitch to the width of the yarn. Secure the zigzag stitch at the beginning and stitch the yarn in place, following a pleasing, natural curve that runs off the side of the quilt.

Adding Borders

There are endless ways to border a quilt both in traditional and contemporary styles. It's important to take time to determine the most unique way to finish each quilt you create. Using many different fabrics for texture and using a change of value to emphasize the border are both terrific ways to add visual impact to the finished piece.

Creating my randomly pieced borders in darker values is one idea. Another dramatic finish is to asymmetrically border some of your pieces by placing the border on only two sides of the quilt rather than all four. Other ideas include:

- Consider using a large-scale fabric for a border of 2½"–3" to create great movement.
- You might decide that a border is not needed; instead, use a bold print for the binding.
- Try creating a yarn binding for a perfect finish (see Yarn Binding, page 32).

In the end, just remember to enjoy experimenting with a few different edging techniques before you make your final decision.

Random-Pieced Border

There are many techniques to strip piecing a border, but the one I like best is to cut out odd-length pieces and sew them back together. This is the traditional method of piecing rather than doing strip sets. It allows me to be more random in the placement of my different fabrics, resulting in a more spontaneous and interesting finished piece. In my *Pink Coneflower #2* quilt, I have a random-pieced border in variations of pinks, all of which are a lighter value than the segmented brown of the quilt top. In my *Remembering...in the Spring* quilt, you will see that I've done my randomly pieced borders in darker values, which effectively sets off the inner design. See Chapter 5 (page 97) for more details.

Here is how to create a randomly pieced border:

1. Use 7–10 fabrics of similar value—probably medium-dark to dark (whatever is a greater contrast to your quilt top). Include different scale prints—small, medium, and large. Confirm that the value and contrast of your choices will be effective with the body of the quilt. Cut three different-size strip sets from each of the different fabrics. For example, 1", 1½", and 2".

2. Cut strips apart crosswise in odd lengths such as 2", 3½", 4", 5½", and 7". Lay the different odd lengths out in random order, keeping the same widths together. Sew strips back together. *Note:* Now, one border might have the 1" random strip in the inner spot, the 2½" strip next, and the 2" strip on the outside. The next border to be attached would have different width strips stitched back together in an alternate order.

3. Before attaching the strip-pieced border to the quilt, trim the strip slightly so it is the same width along its whole length. Border widths are a personal choice, but a larger quilt will have better visual balance with a larger border.

The Tiny Tuck

Now for one additional touch of color—the tiny tuck.

Use a lively fabric that has a bold splash of color. Cut a ¾" strip, the length of your border. If necessary, piece several strips together to reach the length of your border.

Fold the strip in half and press with the iron. When it is time to sew the border (or just the binding) to the quilt, sew the tiny tuck into the seam at the same time. When completed, the tiny tuck will be only a ¼" contrast of color showing.

Look for the tiny tuck feature in orange on *W.B.B.—Wendella B. Butterfly* in Chapter 6 (page 115), in *Remembering...In the Spring* (page 28), and in *Little Gardener III* in Chapter 5 (page 70).

Pink Coneflower #2 has a random pieced border made with various strip widths and length sizes. The border contrasts with the quilt top since the fabrics are different values.

Fig. 8

A splash of color was added to *Remembering...in the Spring* by using a tiny tuck of an irregular striped lime green and black fabric sewn in at the same time as the border strips.

Machine Quilting

Supplies

- Batting: 100 percent cotton
- Binding clips: large, heavy duty (4–12, depending upon quilt size)
- Darning foot and/or walking foot
- Fabric: border (optional); backing
- Fusible stabilizer (for borders)
- Picture image quilt top
- Rotary cutter, mat, and ruler
- Safety pins: 1½" (50–100)
- Threads: assorted for machine quilting

Instructions

1. Carefully and thoroughly press your machine-appliquéd and embellished project. Use the ruler and rotary cutter to trim edges and square corners to prepare for layering (Fig. 8).

2. Add a border if desired. (I wait until the center image of my project is complete before deciding on my border fabric.) Audition numerous fabrics to determine which one works best to enhance overall project. Fuse stabilizer to back of border fabric so entire project has same weight and feel.

3. Cut backing and batting about 1½" larger than appliquéd top on all sides.

4. Sandwich the three layers, clipping each layer onto your worktable with large binder clips as you go. Smooth backing wrong side up; clip. Center batting on backing, smooth, and clip. Layer quilt top right side up, centering it on batting; smooth, and then clip with other layers.

5. Pin-baste by placing safety pins about 4"–5" apart over entire quilt. Consider where you will quilt and avoid placing pins over seams you will be stitching.

Machine Quilting Your Quilt

Until now, you have only completed your sandwiched quilt top. A quilt is not a quilt until the three layers are stitched together. My preferred method for quilting is by machine. I have practiced a great deal and feel comfortable with my techniques, but I know there is always room for refinement.

Machine quilting adds the final touch to a project by creating the textural third dimension, and by enhancing the already wonderful fabrics with quilting lines and threads.

Your project can be quilted with a walking foot using simple stitch-in-the-ditch methods. If you are comfortable with free-motion, you can quilt using a free-motion darning foot and introduce a variety of specialty threads for added complexity.

The secret to machine quilting is to spread the quilting evenly over the quilt surface. If quilting stitches are close together in one section, repeat that density across the rest of the quilt. Don't forget to machine quilt areas that have been embellished. Use similar or complementary thread, continuing to be conscious of the density of your quilting. The goal is for the project to lie flat when you are finished.

I typically begin by stitching in the ditch with the free-motion darning foot across the body of the quilt to stabilize it. Once the project is stabilized, I remove the basting pins. This provides open spaces to do overall specialty quilting.

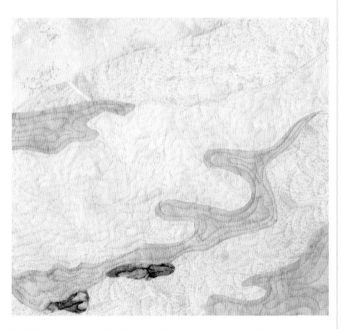

Swirling motions of *Solitude* depict water, whether it be the ocean or a mountain stream. There are so many thread choices to consider. Decide whether you want a light or dark contrasting value, and think about where the light source would hit the water.

Choosing Your Batting

I prefer 100 percent cotton batting that is needle-punched with scrim. This batting can be left unquilted up to 5" or 6" or can be quilted as closely as ½", depending on desired effect.

Stitching How-To

Stitching in the ditch: With a polyester or nylon monofilament thread in the top and bobbin of the machine and a free-motion darning foot in place, stitch in the ditch around large design elements. This stabilizes the three layers to prevent shifting and allows you to remove basting pins. It also outlines key design elements and helps those elements visually pop, adding more dimension to the design.

Overall Specialty Quilting: Once basting pins are removed, you can complete the overall specialty quilting. Focus on one section at a time, and choose threads and quilting designs that complement the fabrics and design element in that section. I use a variety of colorful rayon and trilobal polyester threads to add luminous sheen.

Finishing Techniques

Once the machine quilting is completed, trim the batting and backing flush with the edge of the quilt top. Now you are ready to add a rod pocket, bind your quilt, and add a label.

Supplies

- Fabric: for rod pocket, binding, and label
- Freezer paper
- Hanging rod
- Iron and ironing board
- Needle
- Pins: straight
- Rotary cutter, mat, and ruler
- Scissors: fabric
- Thread: to match sleeve, binding, and label; polyester or cotton

Attaching a Rod Pocket

Instructions

1. Cut rod pocket fabric 9" x width of quilt. Use same or similar fabric as used for quilt backing.

2. Fold each 9" end under ¼", and then ¼" again; sew close to folded edge.

3. Fold rod pocket in half lengthwise, wrong sides together, aligning raw edges. Stitch with ¼" seam.

4. Center stitched seam to back of tube; press. Center and pin upper pressed edge along top back edge of quilt. This edge will be secured with binding. Once binding is in place, fold tube up upon itself approximately ¼"; press and pin.

5. Hand stitch bottom of tube to back of quilt.

Drill a hole at each end of a dowel or slatted stick and use nails to hang the finished quilt.

Double-Fold Binding

Cut binding strips 2¼" wide on the straight grain of the fabric. I use a walking foot and machine stitch the binding to the back of the quilt first, then fold the binding over and top stitch it to the front of the quilt.

1. Measure each side of your quilt and total these measurements. Divide the total by 42" (fabric width) and add a few inches; the resulting number is the number of strips to cut.

2. Join strips with diagonal seams to make one continuous binding strip (Fig. 9). Trim seams to ¼" and press.

Fig. 9

3. Fold starting end of long strip to wrong side, creating 45-degree angle (Fig. 10). Press and trim excess to ¼".

Fig. 10

4. With wrong sides together, fold and press binding strip.

5. With raw edges aligned, attach and pin folded end of binding about 4" from upper back corner of quilt. Use a walking foot to begin stitching about 2" from end of strip, sewing through all three layers with a ¼" seam allowance.

6. Stitch to ¼" from first corner of quilt, stop, pivot, and stitch at a diagonal to corner of quilt (Fig. 11). Remove from machine.

Fig. 11

7. Fold binding strip up, creating diagonal fold. While holding diagonal fold in place, fold binding strip back down over itself, flush with top edge of quilt (Fig. 12).

Fig. 12

8. Resume stitching ¼" from the end of the quilt (Fig. 13) with a ¼" seam allowance around all sides of quilt, turning corners as described.

Fig. 13

9. When you reach the starting point, overlap tail of binding strip about 1½" over beginning of binding. Trim and tuck tail into beginning fold (Fig. 14). Finish sewing binding to quilt and secure final stitches with backstitching.

Fig. 14

10. Fold binding to front of quilt, making sure to cover stitching line. Miter each corner by folding one side of binding over to meet stitching line (Figs. 15 and 16). Fold adjacent side over at a 45-degree angle. Pin and steam press slightly to hold miter in place.

11. Top stitch around entire binding, close to folded edge (Fig. 17). Choose your top thread to blend with background color of binding or use polyester or nylon monofilament thread. Use monofilament thread in bobbin.

Fig. 15

Fig. 17

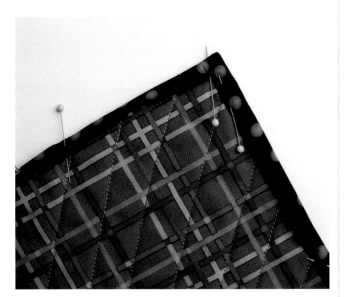

Fig. 16

Yarn Binding

Here is an idea for a unique, speedy, and textural finish to a small wall quilt, using a yarn binding technique:

1. Layer and quilt your small wall quilt. Then, with a rotary cutter, trim all three layers flush with each other. Trim quilt with straight edges or with a bit of an undulating curve.

2. Attach a darning foot to your machine and thread with a monofilament thread. Consider a yarn that is darker or lighter in value than the quilt; one with a fuzzy texture; or a group of yarns that capture some of the colors in the quilt.

3. Once you have chosen the yarn that complements your quilt, take a single strand or multiple strands twisted together and attach yarn to edge of quilt with the widest zigzag stitch. (I prefer a thicker grouping of yarns so they stand up better next to the edge of the quilt.)

4. Hold yarn next to quilt edge and catch both yarn and quilt edge with the wide zigzag. As you start, leave a 1" tail of yarn and zigzag in place to secure it. If you are twisting multiple yarns together, twist a few inches at a time, stitch, then stop and twist some more, then continue to stitch. Stitch all the way around quilt and when you come back to the starting point, trim the beginning 1" tail off; continue overlapping yarn about ½", then trim again.

5. Stitch around the quilt edge twice with the wide zigzag to be sure *all* quilt layers and yarns are securely fastened.

For another idea on yarn binding, take a peek at the *Solitude* quilt in Chapter 6.

Yarn binding in *Little Gardener II* gives a nice finish.

Jot Down the Doodles

I keep a notebook of doodles to refer to when working on quilting designs. Since I have completed many projects, I have developed a number of designs I reuse in modified forms from quilt to quilt.

Labeling Your Quilt

Be sure to create a label with your name, the name of the quilt, and when it was made. For added interest, include a short story about the quilt and its recipient. Some quilters include a few details about the techniques used to make the quilt.

Quilt labels can be printed by hand onto fabric with a permanent fabric marker. Labels can also be created using a document written on your word-processing software and printed onto fabric with a copier or printer.

Choose a very light-colored fabric for your label. Cut a piece of freezer paper to measure exactly 8½" x 11". Iron the freezer paper shiny side down onto the back of the label fabric, and use your rotary cutter and ruler to trim the fabric to the edges of the freezer paper.

Before using the computer for label making, check the colorfastness of your copier or printer ink. Many black ink-jet inks are permanent, but do test your system first.

Turn the edges of the finished quilt label under ¼" and hand stitch to the back corner of the quilt.

I like to create a photo transfer of the original photograph that inspired the quilt and add the transfer to the back of the quilt. The process is easy. Copy the photo to a special photo-transfer fabric, turn the fabric edges under, and hand stitch next to the label in the lower back corner of the quilt.

Place a quilt label and photo transfer from the original photograph along the lower edge of the quilt. Traditionally the label is placed on the lower right corner as the back of the quilt faces you.

CHAPTER THREE

Making Faces

We will study how light and shadow inspire segmenting of the face, and how to use fabric to accomplish the visual look you want.

As you create your photo album quilts, you will at some point encounter the challenge of portraying the human figure, especially the expressive face. When I embarked on my quest to find my voice and my confidence level in working with the face, I studied how other artists of all mediums portray their subjects. Using the photograph to trace from gives me an initial line drawing to work with, but it does have its limitations.

Getting a crisp tracing of eyes and other detailed features can be tricky, so I have used other resources to help me "see" better. Art books and drawing classes, coupled with a great deal of experimentation, have helped me refine my tracings along the way.

In this chapter, I will take you through some of the experimenting processes and describe the discoveries I have made. Careful line drawings, working with fusible web for the facial design elements, and finishing with a bit of thread embellishing all contribute to my successful formula.

Study Before Drawing

I've made many discoveries while experimenting with faces and working to refine the human form in my quilts. Here I will share some of the discoveries and processes I have found particularly helpful.

First and foremost, practice being a keen observer of your surroundings. When you are in a group chatting with others, take time to study their faces. What do eyes really look like? How many parts are there in a nose, or a mouth? To improve your skills in working with the human form, you may wish to seek out a beginning figurative drawing class; I also recommend the book, "Drawing on the Right Side of the Brain" by Betty Edwards.

Original photo

Line drawing

Original photo

Line drawing

Original photo

Line drawing

Using a photograph of my sister, Mary, on her 40th birthday, I experimented with segmenting the face and playing with fabric shadowing.

Original photo   Line drawing

Face Drawings

I chose a variety of photographs that were cropped around the faces and practiced doing line drawings. For many of the exercises, the process went no further than the drawing. I decided it was safer to use photos from outside the immediate family to avoid the critical eye. Exercises included photos of myself, a friend, and my sister.

I selected two of the line drawings and transformed them into fabric. I needed to experiment with segmenting my design to interpret the shadows and creases in each face.

Since I was just playing, I kept going with the idea of using some wacky fabrics for my hair and face. Some great chuckles were coming from the studio now!

When we allow ourselves to work in a spontaneous fashion, it allows our mind to venture further outside its traditional boundaries. Often when our mind is free to wander, some of our best ideas come to life.

As I played with my portrait and my sister's, I dreamed of a wonderful quilt revolving around the theme of "We Become our Mother," illustrating the comment that by the time a woman realizes that her mother was usually right, she has a daughter that thinks she is usually wrong. I visualized portraying my mother, my sister, my daughter, and myself in one quilt around that theme of mothers and daughters. Alas, that quilt hasn't become a reality...yet.

More experimenting on my own face with fabric shadowing.

What would it look like if I used floral fabrics for a more abstract look?

A detail from *Grandma's Little Gardener* shows how the delicate outline of my daughter Emily's profile was lost after tracing it from the original Master Image Map.

Enlarging the Master Image Map can distort the subtler design lines.

Emily's delicate profile as captured on *Little Gardener I*.

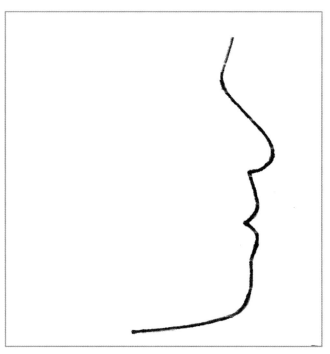

What the profile should have looked like, with more definition around the nose and lips.

Defining Profiles

When I enlarge my original line drawings, not only does the design get bigger, but the tracing lines become fatter. The thickness of the line can increase to about ⅛". This may not seem like an issue, but I discovered that, in fact, it *was* as I created my daughter's profile on my freezer paper template. As I studied the completed quilt with one of my mentors, I asked why the figure did not seem to look "right." She pointed out that the detail of the cute little nose and the line creating Emily's lips had been lost. I had traced the profile on the outside of the thick copy line and lost some of its intricate curves.

From this experience, I began training my eyes to scrutinize what I was tracing more carefully, and I advise you to do the same. Sometimes the original photograph does not have enough contrast for the facial features to show clearly, so as you trace, stand back and take a close look to make sure your tracing is in proportion.

Facial Features

One question often raised when working with the human figure is whether to use recognizable facial features, or to create a more impressionistic form with a faceless figure. I have experimented both ways and have found that when

the scale of the face is smaller, I can get away without facial features. One technique that works well is to use a mottled fabric that already includes a lot of shadowing. I simply take the face template and move it around on the fabric until I find a pleasing spot with the shadows in the right spots. It might be a fleck of shadow where the eyes would be, or a darker swirl in the cheek area.

When we look at a picture of a person, our minds automatically see the human features, whether they are there or not. In addition, we expect to see the features in proportion; if we don't, we may respond negatively. Because of these expectations, it is a real challenge to portray people in artwork.

I decided to embellish eye features in *Grandma's Little Gardener* since the head in this design was of a larger scale. If you take a second look at the other *Little Gardener* quilts featured in Chapter 5, you will realize there are no actual faces.

The size of the face in *Exchanging Gifts—Frog* is small and intricate enough so that it doesn't need any feature details.

When placing a template use subtle shading in the mottled fabric to gently suggest the eye, cheekbone, or mouth.

Go for Contrast

When auditioning fabrics for the face and background, be sure the face fabric contrasts with the lightest sections of the background fabric.

Enlarging the Design

In my quilt, *Remembering...in the Spring*, the size of Verna Mae's face is fairly large. I experimented with segmenting the face along the cheekbone, wondering whether I needed the segmented line for emphasis, or whether I could use my mottled fabric to get the shading I needed. I tried two different fabrics and two different segmentations.

I finally went back to using just one fabric for the face and found enough shading options within the fabric to create the look I was seeking (see page 39).

I traced all the facial features onto my freezer paper template (Fig. 1). As I worked with the eyeglasses, I realized I needed to complete the eyes first, then stitch the eyeglasses.

Fig. 1

Fig. 2

Fig. 3

Fig. 4

Transferring and Embellishing Features

There are several steps I use for transferring the facial features from the original image map to my fabric. This process is ideal for any project where the face is of larger proportion and prominent in the design.

1. Glue appliqué the complete figure.

2. Remove the freezer paper from the top of the fabric and place the part of quilt with the face on a light box, window, or some other backlit source.

3. Place original freezer paper template with facial features (Fig. 1) on the light source behind face on the quilt. With a blue water-soluble disappearing pen, trace facial features (Fig. 2).

4. Choose fabrics for facial features such as eyes, eyebrows, lips, and so on. Trace facial features from freezer paper template onto paper-backed fusible web (Fig. 3).

5. Cut out fusible web tracings with a ¼" seam allowance all around. Bond tracings to back of chosen fabrics, and then cut out on lines.

6. Place fused fabric over traced lines on face; bond in place with iron.

7. Once your whole quilt top has been fused to the fusible stabilizer, machine embellish facial features with different decorative threads (Fig. 4).

8. If the subject wears eyeglasses, trace and stitch them by machine after you have embellished the eyes (Fig. 5).

Fig. 5

Original photo

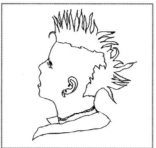
Line drawing

Repetition as a Design Element

Repetition is one of several important design elements used in creating art whether it be a painting, a traditional pieced quilt, or a photo album quilt. It is fun to take the design element of repetition and a specific shape and see what happens. The options are nearly endless. I thought it would be a good exercise to illustrate.

You repeat a shape, a color, or the placement of the shape within the design to create continuity. The ways of doing it vary widely. I decided to play with the repetition of a shape and push myself to work more abstractly.

I was still honing my photo album quilting skills when this idea struck me. I needed to create a quilt for a competition that centered on the theme of color. I chose to use the silhouette line drawing from one of my photographs and challenge myself to work in abstract with the design element of repetition. The photograph was of my son, then 15 and sporting a mohawk.

After much experimenting, I came up with many different designs including this one (Fig. 6).

Fig. 6

"What if I added color?" I thought to myself. I used colored pencils on one of the other designs to decide how I would interpret it in color (Fig. 7).

Fig. 7

I went back to the single silhouette and experimented with two different-colored pencil renderings (Fig. 8).

Fig. 8

After several days and many different design options later, I still did not know which way to go. Cold feet stepped in and the 50" quilt never materialized. The deadline came and went and I had to move on. Later on, I went back to my designs and created a small quilt (see *I Am*, page 116). Sometimes the creative process cannot be forced. I have found that if I let a design idea sit for a time that my mind subconsciously continues to work through possible design options. Then, suddenly, the inspiration hits and I can move forward with the new idea.

CHAPTER FOUR

Project Quilts to Make

A coneflower and a child dreaming of the future are the subjects for you to try now, using the step-by-step picture image appliqué process.

To create a quilt, we need to see something that inspires us. These inspirations will be different for each person, but I have found that flowers and children seem to strike a universal chord.

I love flowers and believe they speak to every heart. Flowers are always perfect for beginners because they have simple, beautiful shapes. Whether the flower image is of a geranium, daisy, poinsettia, hibiscus, or daffodil, any one of them could be a picture image appliqué project.

Capturing a child in a quilt design is a bit more challenging, but the rewards are tremendous. Children are naturally curious, spontaneous, gleeful, fun loving, and creative.

To get you started, here are three projects with detailed instructions. You will ultimately want to use your own images, but these instructions will give you an introduction to the process, work you through the steps, and give you the confidence to venture out on your own.

Pink Coneflower #1

Of all the blooms I have in my garden, the pink coneflower is one of my favorites. This flower has special meaning for me since it is one my mother grew in her own summer prairie garden in Wisconsin. After she died, the pink coneflower and others continued to live on and I continue to transplant the flower lovingly into friends' gardens as well as my own.

I chose to work with the coneflower first because of the many memories it evokes but also because the shape of the large center and elongated petals allowed me to create a simple line drawing for the design.

I have many photos of the coneflower. When I created the line drawing, I followed the same lines as the flower in the photo below, but drew fewer petals to simplify the image.

Line drawing

Detail of pink coneflower used in pattern.

Original photo

Tools

- Adhesives: cellophane tape, masking tape, and white glue sticks (2–3)
- Darning foot (free-motion foot) or zigzag foot for machine appliqué
- Darning foot (free-motion foot) or walking foot for machine quilting
- Iron and ironing board
- Rotary cutter, mat, and ruler
- Scissors: fabric and paper
- Sewing machine
- Stiletto or other sharp tool

Supplies

- Fabric
- Freezer paper (2 sheets)
- General sewing supplies
- Markers: extra/ultra-fine permanent in black, blue, green, and red
- Straight pins
- Threads: polyester or nylon monofilament in clear and smoke for machine appliqué

Pink Coneflower #1, 15" x 21"

Selecting Fabrics

Visit your stash and choose the fabrics for your flower. Fan out your options, then step back to see how they work together.

Select a few options for your whole-cloth background but wait until the flower is completed before making the final decision for the background. Pin your background fabric to the design board and put the flower fabrics on top to be sure there is enough contrast. Keep these tips in mind when choosing your fabric for the *Pink Coneflower #1* quilt (and by the way, it doesn't have to be pink).

Flower: Create whatever flower color you wish—blue, pink, purple, red, or yellow. If you choose a dark background as shown, you will want to choose medium to medium-light values for the flower, leaves, and stem. If you use a light background, your flower fabric will need to be darker in value. I used:

- Flower center: medium value fabric; small 5" scrap
- Flower petals: large scraps (6" square) of 5–6 fabrics of similar value
- Flower stem and leaves: fat quarter, medium to light green or brown

Background:

- ⅝ yard hand dyed, tone-on-tone, mottled fabric. Background should contrast with the flower fabrics.
- ⅝ yard fusible stabilizer

Border:

- ½ yard; consider a large print

Master Image Map Enlarging

This original copy with all its labeled and marked pattern pieces (page 47) will be your Master Image Map and will guide you as you glue appliqué your template sections back together. For a 14" x 18" flower, enlarge 200 percent; for 18" x 23", enlarge 255 percent.

Finishing the Quilt

- 24" x 27" batting, 100 percent cotton with scrim
- 24" x 27" fabric for backing, label, rod pocket
- ¼ yard binding
- Threads: specialty threads, rayons, metallics, cottons, and monofilament for machine quilting

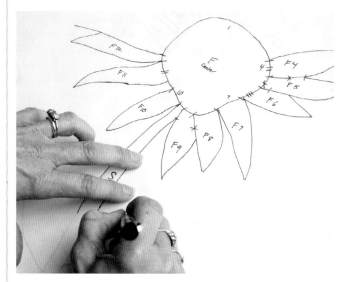

Fig. 1

Preparing Freezer Paper Templates

1. Cut freezer paper 1½" larger than Master Image Map on all sides. If the freezer paper is not wide enough, piece paper together with a solid strip of masking tape, overlapping each sheet about ½" (masking tape will not melt under the iron). Be sure the freezer paper is shiny side *down* when placing it over your Master Image Map; center it and tape down the corners.

2. Using black permanent marker, trace all lines of the Master Image Map onto the freezer paper (Fig. 1). Be sure to label all the pieces and include the tic marks and the labeling system. To differentiate the markings, label the tic marks with colored extra-fine permanent markers (blue or green) and the slash marks at the junctions in red (Fig. 2).

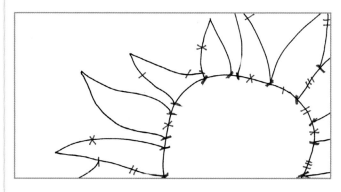

Fig. 2

Master Image Map

14" x 18": enlarge 200%
18" x 23": Enlarge 255%

Labeling Chart
F = Flower and Petals
   (add numerals for each
      piece: 1, 2, 3, 4 etc.)
S = Stem
L = Leaves

Cutting Templates and Attaching to Fabric

1. Cut out your paper template pieces (Fig. 3). Be sure to follow black lines as exactly as possible.

2. Iron template onto front side of fabric, allowing for an approximate ¼" seam allowance all around. Iron with a hot steam iron for several seconds to adhere the freezer paper to the fabric (Fig. 4).

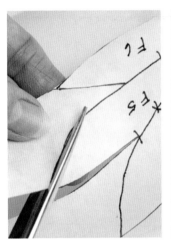

Fig. 3

Fig. 4

3. Cut fabric with a ¼" seam allowance all around—no larger or it will be difficult to turn fabric under (Fig. 5).

4. Clip fabric every ½"–1" around concave and convex curves for easier turning (Fig. 6).

Fig. 5

Fig. 6

Template Gluing Techniques

Cover your worktable with a plain piece of paper to catch surplus glue stick. Line up template pieces in order on your worktable (Fig. 7).

There are two types of edges we can create with our appliqué: turned under and raw edge. For general directions, refer to Assembling Template Pieces in Chapter 2 (pages 21 and 22). For *Pink Coneflower #1*, we'll proceed here with the turned-under technique and describe the raw-edge alternative at the end of this section.

Fig. 7

1. Turn over flower petal piece F1 to the back of the fabric. Swipe glue along edge F1A and press fabric so it folds and is glued back on itself, flush along the freezer paper edge (Figs. 8 and 9). For a nice point, trim fabric straight across, close to point of template, then trim the corner of edge F1B about ⅛" (Fig. 10).

Fig. 8

Fig. 9

Fig. 10

2. Swipe glue along edge 1B petal and press fabric so it folds back under, flush along freezer paper edge in the same way as edge 1A (Figs. 11 and 12). Repeat process for petals F2 and F3. For F4, clip at slash mark on edge F4A and glue seam flush with freezer paper from slash mark to tip of petal (Fig. 13). At the tip, trim fabric straight across, close to point of template, then trim corner of edge F4B about ⅛". The whole edge of F4B will be glued flush with freezer paper as done for F3.

from slash mark to tip (Fig. 13). Join those touching by placing glue on the remaining open seam allowance and snuggle with adjoining flower petal.

4. Once petals are complete (Fig. 14), clip flower center seam allowance (Fig. 15), glue, and turn seam all around flush with freezer paper edge.

5. Join petals to flower center following numbering and tic markings indicated on flower petals.

6. Add leaves and stem. Stem edges will be completely turned under except at the spot where the stem joins the flower. The leaves will also be turned under except where they join the stem. While working, keep glued sections fairly flat to allow glue to set.

Fig. 11   Fig. 12

3. Place glue on open ¼" seam allowance from base of flower petal to slash mark on F4A (right side of fabric) and snuggle it next to F3, matching tic marks and slashes. Continue with each flower petal by clipping at slash marks and gluing seams flush with freezer paper

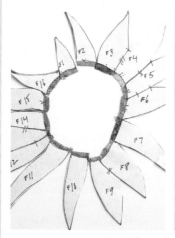

Fig. 14

Fig. 15

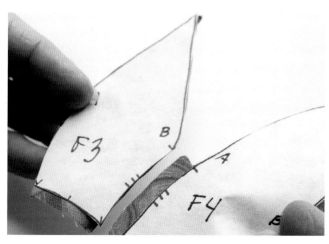

Fig. 13

Perfect Placement

To mark which fabric will go where in the pattern, you can either cut a tiny swatch and tape the fabric in the desired location on your Master Image Map or jot down the numbered sections to coordinate with the fabric on a piece of paper and pin it to the fabric.

Edging Your Bets

The secret to deciding which kind of edging technique to use—turned under versus raw—is to understand the different effect each one gives.

An advantage to using the turned-under edge is that as in traditional needle-turn appliqué, the turned-under edge will give the design element added dimension and a more formal finish. A turned-under edge on all exterior edges of the design provides extra visual dimension.

The first advantage to raw-edge finishing is that the process is much faster. Also, a raw edge offers more texture; you might use it to give the edge of a flower a softer finish.

When using a raw edge, it's nice to go back and do additional machine embellishing over those edges with a variety of threads. More about this process is discussed in Machine Embellishing in Chapter 2 (pages 24 and 25).

Combining turned-under edge and raw-edge techniques works well, too. When using both methods, I often use the raw edge on interior joined seams and at tricky junctures. I then use the turned-under edge for my exterior seams joined on the background for the added dimension it offers.

Fig. 16

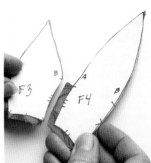

Fig. 17

Gluing Process for Raw Edge Alternative

For a raw edge finish, take the F1 template and trim seam allowance A and B *flush* with the freezer paper (Fig. 16).

For template parts such as petals and leaves that join together, trim the fabric to the edge of the freezer paper on F4 side A from the tip of the petal down to the slash mark on F4 (Fig. 17). Swipe the glue stick along the ¼" seam allowance on F4 side A and snuggle it along the F3 template raw edge of seam allowance B. *Note:* For template parts that join together be sure to leave the ¼" seam allowance on one of the templates so the pieces can be joined together.

Continue to work in sections until the whole design is glued together. Once completed, all you see are the freezer paper templates with fabric hidden underneath (Fig. 18).

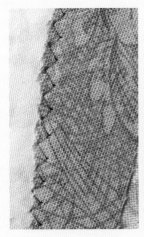

Detail of raw edge with machine appliqué

Detail of turned-under edge with machine appliqué

Fig. 18

Fig. 19

Peeking Under the Freezer Paper

Once you have allowed the glue to set up briefly, remove the freezer paper and view your coneflower (Fig. 19).

Stand back and evaluate your fabric choices. Once you are satisfied with how the fabrics coordinate in the flower, leave the freezer paper off and finalize your whole-cloth background fabric.

Fig. 20   Fig. 21

Creating the Background

Remember that auditioning several different backgrounds is a fun exercise. Pin the possible background fabrics to the design board and pin the glued pink coneflower on top, checking for contrast and visual interest.

Once background fabric is chosen, cut it about 1" larger than your finished piece and back it with fusible stabilizer (Fig. 20).

Dab glue stick in several spots on back of flower and attach flower to the stabilized background fabric to temporarily hold it in place.

Time To Machine Appliqué

Thread top of machine with clear monofilament thread for light fabrics, smoke thread for dark fabrics. In the bobbin, use a neutral color thread or monofilament.

Using either a darning foot or a regular zigzag foot, machine appliqué each of the glued edges into place (Fig. 21). Set the stitch width to 1.5 for turned-under edges, 2.0 for raw edges.

Adding the Border

Audition border fabrics next and when you have made your choice, cut strips 2¼" wide.

Attach the borders with a ¼" seam allowance and press. Next, take the fusible stabilizer and cut strips 2" wide. At the ironing board, lay the quilt top face down and place the stabilizer on the border fabrics and fuse in place. Adding the stabilizer to the border fabric will create equal weight over the whole surface of the quilt.

Preparing Project for Quilting

To prepare your backing fabric and batting, cut backing and batting about 1½" larger than appliquéd top. Sandwich the three layers and pin baste for machine quilting. Refer to Chapter 2 (page 28) for details.

Machine Quilting

Stabilize the quilt by stitching in the ditch around the flower (Fig. 22). This can be done best with the darning foot using monopoly thread in the top and in the bobbin.

Quilt the background. Stitch in the ditch around the seam allowance at the border, then quilt in the border (Fig. 23).

Bind and label your quilt, referring to Finishing Techniques in Chapter 2 (pages 30-32) for details.

Fig. 22   Fig. 23

Pink Coneflower #2

Pink Coneflower #2 is a variation of *Pink Coneflower #1*. Using the same original photograph, I simply chose different fabrics and stitch patterns.

This pattern will give you practice in creating a segmented background around your primary design element. The segmented background can offer a greater sense of complexity to the overall project and will give you the challenge of coordinating additional fabrics together with a simple pattern.

Tools and Supplies

Refer to the lists under Pink Coneflower #1 on page 44.

Give Yourself Some Space

It's good to have 1"–1½" of extra space around the outside of the quilt top so that once the edges are trimmed and corners squared, you do not have to trim into the body of the quilt.

Removing Glue

Occasionally, you will put the glue on the wrong side of the fabric. When this happens, either let it air dry or use a hot iron on the glue and it will dry immediately so you can then re-glue correctly.

Selecting Fabric

Flower: Refer to Selecting Fabrics on page 46.

Segmented background: Three fat quarters of fabrics of similar value. Hand-dyed look, tone on tone, mottled look, small print. Background should contrast with the fabrics for the flower.

A random pieced border was used on this quilt.

Optional random pieced border: 6–8 different fabrics of varying scale and prints that pull colors from the center flower. One 1½" strip and one 1¾" strip from each of the 6–8 fabrics chosen. For more details, refer to Random-Pieced Border in Chapter 2 (page 26).

Preparing Freezer Paper Templates

1. Follow all of the directions for *Pink Coneflower #1*. When you trace the Master Image Map, include the segmenting lines and tic marks for the background on your freezer paper templates. For 10" x 17", enlarge 200 percent; 12" x 21¼", enlarge 250 percent; 15" x 25½", enlarge 300 percent.

Pink Coneflower #2, 17" x 22"

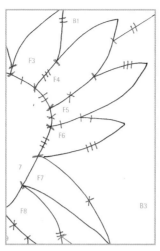

Fig. 24   Fig. 25   Fig. 26   Fig. 27

2. Trace your Master Image Map to freezer paper image map, being sure to leave an extra 1"–1½" around the outside of the freezer paper (Fig. 24).

3. Cut out flower on tracing lines and save the background templates. The background template pieces and flower pieces have tic marks to guide flower into correct position on segmented background (Fig. 25). *Note:* When flower is glued together, do not remove the freezer paper.

Segmented Background

1. Choose background fabrics. Iron freezer paper templates onto fabric; cut out with ¼" seam allowance all around.

2. Begin assembling background segments together. Glue one seam and fold under flush with freezer paper edge; leave next seam open. Swipe glue along open seam and snuggle folded edge seam on top, matching tic marks.

3. Continue piecing the background segments together. At the end, there is a space to place the flower (Fig. 26).

4. Using the glue stick, glue ¼" seam allowances of the background pieces and place the flower into its spot matching the tic marks on the flower petals with the tic marks on the background templates. Allow the glued pieces to dry a few minutes before handling.

5. Before removing all of the freezer paper, take a few pieces off to confirm that the value choices for the flower against the background values work effectively (Fig. 27). You can also turn the project over and look at the back of the fabrics to get a sense of how it will look. Since the project is small, a third way to check is to hold the glued project up to a back lighting source, a window, or lamp and take a peek.

6. When you are ready, remove the freezer paper, iron the glue appliquéd piece onto the fusible stabilizer, and machine appliqué the glued edges.

7. Quilt and bind your quilt (Fig. 28).

Fig. 28—Examples of machine quilting on *Pink Coneflower #2*

Master Image Map

10" x 17": enlarge 200%
12" x 21¼": enlarge 250%
15" x 25½": enlarge 300%

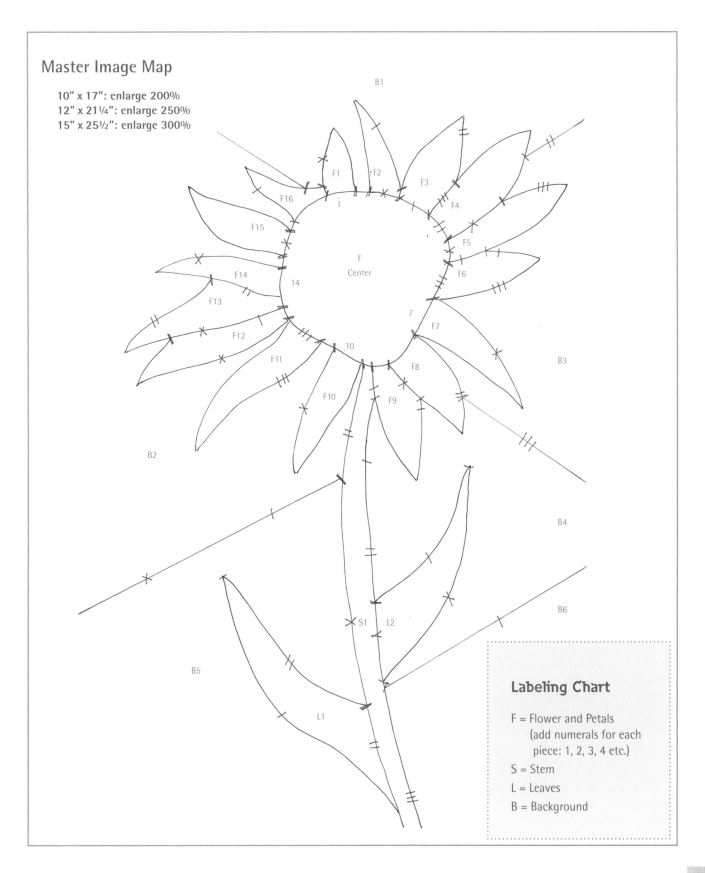

Labeling Chart

F = Flower and Petals
   (add numerals for each
    piece: 1, 2, 3, 4 etc.)
S = Stem
L = Leaves
B = Background

Project 3

Take on the World

This candid photograph of a little Mexican child holding a world balloon evokes powerful images of the many wonderful adventures our children have ahead of them. My brother captured this photo on one of his mission trips to Mexico.

The image contains simple lines for you to begin your journey creating quilts that portray the human figure. The hair, clothing, and skin tone can be chosen to portray the image of a grandchild, a special neighbor down the street, or maybe the child within each of us who is ready to spread his or her wings and take on the world.

Original line drawing

Original photo

Tools

- Adhesives: cellophane tape, masking tape, white glue sticks (2–3)
- Darning foot (free-motion foot) or zigzag foot for machine appliqué
- Darning foot (free-motion foot) or walking foot for machine quilting
- Iron and ironing board
- Rotary cutter, mat, and ruler
- Scissors: fabric and paper
- Sewing machine
- Stiletto or other sharp tool

Supplies

- ½ yard yarn, string, or ribbon for balloon tail
- Extra/ultra-fine permanent markers: black, blue, green, red
- Fabric
- Freezer paper (2 sheets; 15" x 27")
- General sewing supplies
- Straight pins
- Threads: polyester or nylon monofilament in clear and smoke for machine appliqué

Take on the World, 20" x 30"

Selecting Fabrics

Sky: Three fat quarters different light value blues or ½ yard mottled sky blue fabric.

Background: Five fat quarters (one of each) medium to medium dark grays and blue/grays, mixing small, medium, and large prints.

World: One fat quarter medium light value. For the continents, use 8"–10" scrap medium dark value, with medium contrast to the world fabric. For the shadow, use 10" scrap of black fabric (could be the same black fabric used in the hair).

Fabric for Child: For hair, use 5"–6" scraps of four different black fabrics, same values. For shirt, you choose the color. Main part of shirt, use fat quarter medium value. Tucks and folds of shirt, use 8" scrap of darker value. Sleeves and collar of shirt, use 8" scrap of another medium value. For pants, use fat quarter of your choice. For face, arm, and legs, use fat quarter medium to medium light value skin tone. For ear, use scrap one step darker in value than face fabric. For sandals, 6"–8" scrap of dark brown fabric.

Select fabrics for different sections of your quilt. Fan out your fabric options, step back, and see how they work together. Finalize the fabric choices for your child figure. Next, make your choices for the sky and background. Pin background fabrics to the design board and put child fabrics on top to be sure there is enough contrast. Mark placement of the fabric on your Master Image Map.

Enlarging Master Image Map

This original copy with all its labeled and marked pattern pieces (page 59) will be your Master Image Map and will guide you as you glue appliqué template sections back together. For 18" x 23", enlarge 255 percent; for 24" x 31", enlarge 340 percent.

Finishing the Quilt

- ¾ yard batting, 100 percent cotton with scrim
- ¼ yard binding
- ¾ yard fabric for backing and rod pocket
- ¾ yard fusible stabilizer
- Threads: polyester or nylon monofilament in clear and smoke, assorted rayons and metallics for machine embellishing and machine quilting

Preparing Freezer Paper Templates

1. Cut freezer paper 1½" larger than Master Image Map on all sides. If freezer paper is not wide enough, piece paper together with a solid strip of masking tape, overlapping each sheet about ½". Be sure freezer paper is shiny side down when placing it over Master Image Map; center it and tape down corners.

2. Using black marker, trace all lines of the Master Image Map onto the freezer paper. Be sure to label all the pieces and include the tic marks and the labeling system (Fig. 29). As an alternative, to differentiate the markings, label the tic marks with colored markers and the slash marks at junctions in red. Draw a red line around the outside of the pattern, then draw another line an extra 1½" all around. Extend the background lines of your design into the fudge room (see Give Yourself Some Space, page 52).

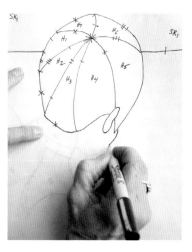

Fig. 29

Labeling Chart

A = Arm	L = Leg
B = Blouse	P = Pants
F = Face	S = Shoes
G = Ground	SK = Sky
H = Hair	W = World

Master Image Map

18" x 23": enlarge 255%
24" x 31": enlarge 340%

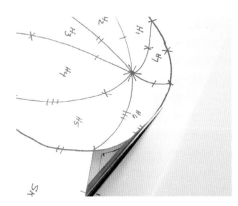

Fig. 30

Assembling Freezer Paper Templates

1. Beginning with central figure, cut out freezer paper figure of child along traced lines as closely as possible (Fig. 30). Place segmented background freezer paper template aside and begin with the central figure first—the head of hair.

2. Cut out hair sections.

Fig. 31   Fig. 32

Reuse Your Paper

You can reuse freezer paper templates up to three times. After that, rub with a sponge lightly on the shiny side of the freezer paper to remove bits of fiber and the templates can be used additional times.

3. With a hot steam iron, press freezer paper template to the *front* side of the fabric and allow ¼" seam allowance all around (Fig. 31). Hold for several seconds to adhere the freezer paper to the fabric. Cut fabric around each template with a ¼" seam allowance. Clip fabric every ½"–1" around concave and convex curves for easier turning (Fig. 32).

Fig. 33   Fig. 34

4. Cover your worktable with a plain piece of paper to catch surplus glue stick. Line the hair template pieces in order on your worktable (Fig. 33).

5. Take hair piece H1 and turn over to the back of the fabric. Swipe glue along edge 1A and press fabric so that it folds and is glued under, flush along the freezer paper edge (Fig. 34).

Fig. 35   Fig. 36

6. Swipe glue along ¼" seam allowance of H2, then snuggle H1 next to H2, matching tic marks (Fig. 35). Continue assembling all hair templates in same manner. Leave outer edges of head for last and turn them all at the same time.

7. In center of the head, there may be a bulk of edges where all points come together. Trim a few of the points underneath to reduce bulk.

8. When all hair templates are glued together, clip seams around outside of head and glue seam under, flush with freezer paper, all the way around head (Fig. 36).

9. Because ear template is small, trim seam allowance to ⅛", clipping closely around curves, then begin gluing. Attach completed ear template to head with a dab of glue stick before stitching, but wait until the end of quilt assembly so it does not get knocked off and lost.

Foreground and Background Seam Finishes

In the majority of cases, seam allowances for foreground pieces will be turned under and seam allowances in the background sections will be kept flat. For example, the hair on the figure is in the foreground and the face and neck are underneath the hair in the background. Thus, the hair template seams are turned under and will snuggle up with the face and neck seams, which are left flat.

Removing Seam Shadows

Occasionally when working with lighter fabrics such as skin tones and the body parts of the face, arms, and legs, the turned-under seam allowances may show through especially if placed against a dark fabric. To resolve this, cut a second template piece of the same fabric with your template pattern and place it under the first piece. Secure in place with a dab of glue stick.

Shirt Assembly

1. Cut shirt templates out next. Use first fabric for main part of shirt. The folds/tucks in the shirt (B4, B6, B7, B10, B12) have a darker value to add depth and dimension. Use third fabric to define the sleeves (B2 and B14) and collar (B1).

2. Take shirt section B3 and glue seam allowance A under. For shirt section B5, glue seam allowance B under, then tuck B4 and swipe glue on open seam allowances. Slide it under B3 and B5, matching tic marks (Fig. 37). Continue with rest of shirt. Wait to turn under all outer seams of shirt at the same time (Fig. 38).

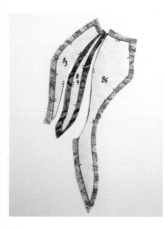

Fig. 37 Fig. 38

Pants Assembly

Assemble pants using same process as shirt. As you cut tuck template for pants, change fabric direction to add visual texture. (If you chose a print or solid fabric instead of a stripe, choose a darker value fabric for the tuck.)

Arm Assembly

Turn under edges along arm template. When you reach fingers, trim that section to ⅛" and clip curves more closely. Clip directly into V where each knuckle is formed. Use your sharp tool to assist in gluing and turning edges around indentations of the knuckles. Refer to Trimming Seams with Ease in Chapter 2 (page 22).

Legs Assembly

Glue edges under, along the templates for the legs; set aside.

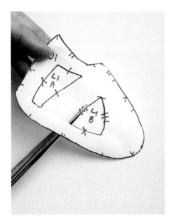

Fig. 39

Fig. 40

Sandals

To retrieve small feet templates included in the sandals, cut along lower section of freezer paper to remove the feet sections L1A, L1B, and L2A (Fig. 39). Press sandal template to sandal fabric with cut section flush together on fabric. Use one of two methods:

Method #1: Turn seam allowances under all the way around the exterior of the sandals as well as the interior seam sections of the sandals where the feet peek through.

Method #2: Turn edges under all the way around the exterior of the sandals. Then trim seam allowances flush with the edge of the freezer paper for interior seam sections, creating a raw edge where the feet fabric will peek through (Fig. 40).

Child Figure Assembly

Once all the sections of the child are complete—head, shirt, pants, arms, and legs—glue each section together and let it sit 10–15 minutes.

The World

Cut out world templates and press them to fabric pieces. Use raw edge for continent templates and turned-under edge for outer edges of world.

Taking a Look

Since your child figure and the world balloon must be placed into center of segmented background, do not take off freezer paper yet. Once glue has set up briefly, carefully hold figure against a sunny window or lamp. The light should reflect through the fabric and freezer paper well enough to give you an idea of how the fabrics are working with each other.

Sky Assembly

Cut out the templates for the sky, iron templates to fabric, and cut out with ¼" seam allowance. Lay sky pieces in order on your worktable and glue appliqué together.

Ground Assembly

Repeat steps from Sky Assembly. When gluing the sky to the ground pieces, remember that the sky falls *behind* the ground. Turn under seam allowances of ground templates, then snuggle them with ¼" open seam allowances of sky.

Final Assembly

A space will be left to insert child figure. Place glue on the ¼" seam allowances of the background pieces and place the child figure into its spot. Allow the glued sections to dry 8–10 minutes before handling.

Taking Another Peek

To see how the figure fabrics work with the background fabrics, take another peek. Once the glue has set a bit, *carefully* hold the glue appliquéd piece up to the light source.

Unveiling the Fabric

Remove all of the freezer paper templates.

Preparing Fusible Stabilizer

Cut a piece of fusible stabilizer to the size of the assembled top minus about ¼" and slip it under project. Pin project to stabilizer in several places along the top and bottom as well as a few pins in the middle. Pin it to the design board for careful scrutiny and to evaluate fabric choices.

Once you are satisfied with your fabric choices, take the project to the ironing board and fuse glue appliquéd quilt top to fusible stabilizer. Work from center out, using a slow tapping motion with hot iron. Hold iron in place 8–10 seconds to activate fusible stabilizer, which does not fuse as quickly as fusible web. As you near the edge of your project, be careful not to let the hot iron touch the fusible stabilizer.

Couching Balloon String

Thread your machine with clear monopoly/monofilament thread. Set the zigzag wide enough to catch each outside edge of the yarn, ribbon, or string.

Lay the yarn in place, holding it with a few pins. Tuck edges of yarn under edges of the child's shirt, hand, and edge of balloon. At the spot where the child is holding the string in his hand, don't run the yarn under the whole hand; instead, tuck ¼" under seam allowance at the top of the hand, and then start up the yarn again by tucking ¼" under seam allowance again at underside of the hand (Fig. 41). Couch in place (Fig. 42).

Fig. 41   Fig. 42

Time to Machine Appliqué

Thread machine with monofilament at top and neutral thread or monofilament in the bobbin. For lighter fabrics, use clear thread; for darker fabrics, use smoke. Set zigzag stitch width to 1.5 for turned-under seams and 2.0 for raw-edge seams. Stitch all glued edges down with zigzag stitch.

Steaming and Trimming

When all the appliqué is completed, steam project well with iron. Then with ruler and rotary cutter, trim edges and square corners to prepare for layering.

Adding a Border

Putting a border on a quilt is a personal choice. I wait to decide what edging my quilt needs once the center is finished. Take time to audition a number of fabrics to see what would work best as a border. Then decide what looks right to you and your project.

If you decide to put a border on your project, refer to the border directions for *Pink Coneflower #1* on page 51. Use a 3"–4" border.

Layering Your Project

Cut backing and batting 1½" larger than quilt top. Follow layering directions in Maching Quilting Your Quilt, page 28), and pin baste.

Machine Quilting

To stabilize project, stitch in the ditch around all edges of figure. Use monofilament in both top of machine and bobbin.

Continue to stitch in the ditch in background as well. More experienced quilters may want to use a darning foot to create added texture with machine quilting stitches.

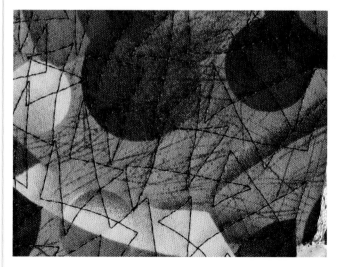

Some of the machine quilting stitches used in *Take on the World*.

CHAPTER FIVE

Tips, Tricks & Tutorials

Some of my best techniques came from trial and error.
I am sharing them here with you to help you build
your own arsenal of creative answers to any design
challenges that may come your way.

You would think that an experienced quilter like me—one who
has made about 250 quilts—would have seen everything, but this
isn't true. The longer I quilt, the more I believe that there will
always be something new to learn and new discoveries to make.

In my workshops and lectures, quilters raise many good questions about
how I reach one design decision or another, or how I create special features
within my quilts. I'm convinced that peeking at another artist's problem-
solving process can help us with our own. So rather than providing complete
step-by-step instructions and/or patterns for many of my quilts, I have chosen
to open up my collection and reveal a few key highlights of the creative
process I worked through to make each piece. In these pages, you will
find hints as to how I resolved a particular design challenge, as
well as a few special techniques that you can add to
your personal repertoire.

Grandma's Little Gardener

I originally created this piece for the annual auction challenge sponsored by the American Quilter's Society. The challenge theme was "Windows."

The photograph of 5-year-old Emily was taken in Grandma Butler's prairie garden in Lake Mills, Wisconsin. Emily was picking flowers during the family's memorial service for my mother. Memories of Grandma and her prairie garden come to my mind every time I see a coneflower bloom. I wanted to capture the beauty and wonder of a little girl's discovery in the flower garden and to suggest a connection from generation to generation. In this quilt, the window of the barn became the place where the spirit of Grandma looks out over us all.

Original photo

Line drawing

Quilter's Notes

I stay focused and excited about every project I work on because I am so anxious to see the outcome. A lot of time and energy went into constructing this quilt. In fact, when it was completed, the quilt held such a personal connection for me that I could not give it up for auction and kept it for my own collection.

Red Barn

Depicting the red barn on our old apple orchard property was great fun, and I had a large collection of red fabrics to choose from. Instead of using the picture-image appliqué process, I decided it would be much more efficient to strip piece my red fabrics together first. I pressed the barn wall freezer paper template to the strip pieced fabric and cut out the barn wall shape. I used this same process for the white clapboard side of the barn, using four different creamy-white fabrics.

Creating a Pattern

From this first depiction of my daughter gathering flowers, a wonderful idea emerged. I found that I could show my students how to start with a simple pattern, to learn my picture-image appliqué technique, and then to turn the pattern into their own unique interpretation with a few color and fabric changes.

From this realization, the pattern, *Little Gardener*, was born. Since that time, hundreds of students have made their own little gardeners, turning the design into a personalized portrait of someone special in their life. A particular hair color, a change of background, or a different shirt makes each design unique.

As I work on quilts, I am always asking myself, "What if?" What if I change the hair color? What if I choose a different background? My students inspired me to create my own variations and they seem to multiply in my closet like fast-growing seeds.

On the following pages are those little gardeners and the things I learned while creating them.

Grandma's Little Gardener, 39" x 30", © 2004

Little Gardener I

18" x 24", © 2004

Little Gardener I is the subject for many workshops I teach and I have such fun using this pattern. The key word is simple. I wanted students to learn the picture-image appliqué technique and have fun with it. The size of the pattern is 18" x 24", a size that works well for an early project, and I simplified lines in the drawing to make it even more suitable.

The hair is segmented into just six pieces, and I selected only a few flowers, enlarging them from the original design for easier manipulation. Placing the glue-appliquéd figure on a whole-cloth background rather than a segmented background simplified things as well.

Quilter's Notes

Whole Cloth Background

This is the first quilt I created with the simplified pattern. The whole-cloth background of hand-dyed fabric was perfect for the coneflowers. The splashes of red were just right to give the feel of a garden in bloom. The hair color, shirt color, and skin tone were all carefully chosen so they would contrast well with the background.

Little Gardener II

24" x 20", © 2004

Once I had a quilt with simple construction lines, I created an example to demonstrate how one can change the pattern and use a segmented background for added interest. The sky and the garden area were segmented in similar fashion to the original *Grandma's Little Gardener* quilt. The figure of the little gardener was assembled first, the segmented background was assembled, and finally, the figure was snuggled into place within the segmented background.

Quilter's Notes

Segmented Background

In areas where my foreground figures—such as the flowers—were small and more intricate, I traced the segmented background of the Master Image Map onto the freezer paper without the foreground flowers. I then glue-appliquéd the background as a single, complete section. Later, I went back and traced the flowers onto a separate sheet of freezer paper, assembled them, and machine appliquéd them on top of the segmented background.

Little Gardener III

23" x 18", © 2004

My little gardener appears once again, this time against a vibrant field of mustard yellow. You can see how endless the possibilities are for even a simple subject, just by changing color, texture, and finishing techniques.

Quilter's Notes

Designing Around Color

The initial choice of a fabric often will dictate the direction of the project. In *Little Gardener III*, I chose the mustard yellow hand-dyed background. This decision, coupled with a desire to experiment, led me to revise my flower colors.

I chose a lighter value of yellow so the coneflowers would contrast with the gold background, and chose purple for the remaining coneflowers. Referring to the color wheel, I saw that yellow and purple are complementary colors, so I knew the combination would work well.

I initially created a dark blue shirt for this little gardener; however, when I joined the blue shirt with the black hair, I realized there was not enough contrast, so I remade the shirt in a new color.

Add Some Jazz

The tiny tuck in this binding is made with a black-and-gold plaid fabric, creating a jazzy finish for the little quilt. See The Tiny Tuck in Chapter 2 (page 27) for details.

Exchanging Gifts—Ice Cream Cone

21" x 17", © 2005

This little gardener has darker hair and darker skin tone, so I was able to place her on a lighter-value, creamy-yellow print background. For this project, I was ready to exchange the flower for something different, and I hit upon the idea of an ice cream cone.

About the only thing I have not yet done with my little gardeners is to name them individually. Each is unique in her or his own way, and each demonstrates the personality of a daughter, granddaughter, niece, nephew, or neighbor's child much like the ones we all have in our lives. Perhaps as we create these little quilted gardeners, they may also evolve unconsciously into the child hidden inside us all.

Quilter's Notes

Quick Change Artistry

I'll admit that I've eaten so many ice cream cones in my life that I could easily draw one without a picture to trace. An ice cream cone is simply an elongated triangle topped with some "lumpy" half circles. I took a piece of copy paper and did some sketching and doodling with a pencil. Then I traced over it with a permanent marker, laid my Master Image Map over my drawing, and traced it in place.

Exchanging Gifts—Frog

21" x 17", © 2005

I love interacting with my students. There is a constant interchange of ideas. I give them tips and techniques to inspire their creativity, but I also receive special gifts from them in return.

There are always students that I teasingly call my "troublemakers" who want to venture from the pattern and do something different. These troublemakers will ask tentatively if they can make changes in the pattern and I answer wholeheartedly, "Yes, of course!" Anytime someone wants to wander down his or her own path, I will assist as best I can.

In one Photo-Album Quilt class, two students wanted to make the figures into little boys, and proceeded to change the hairline of the original pattern. I had considered making a little boy pattern, but had not gotten around to it.

Quilter's Notes

Changing Hairlines

I was inspired by my students to create a little boy outline, so following that workshop, I went home and played with the Little Girl drawing and with a simple change of the hair and adding an ear peeking out, I came up with the Little Boy. Once I had a little boy outline, it was time to create a new quilt featuring a little boy and his frog. The frog was created with fusible web in the same manner as the ice cream cone. Taking a successful design from one of your photos one step further is certainly a challenge you could offer yourself in the future.

Little changes make big differences in photo album quilts. Here, substituting the original flower picking with a leaping frog changes the whole story.

Captivating Coneflower

It amazes me how many quilts have been inspired by one photograph. So many quilters are gardeners, and as I created more patterns using my picture image appliqué process, I found flowers to be a recurring theme.

Once again, the coneflower appears as the star, but now it is enhanced with extra details, including a dragonfly created as its own appliqué to give it added dimension. Lots of thread doodling and a raw-edge finish add to the visual feast.

Original photo

Line drawing

Quilter's Notes
Adding Raw-Edge Flourishes

All the edges of this quilt were created with the raw-edge appliqué process. Since I enjoy machine embellishing as well, I added more texture by doodling with different decorative threads.

I used a wider zigzag stitch to appliqué the raw edge seams in place to prevent the fabric from fraying.

Raw edge seam on petal

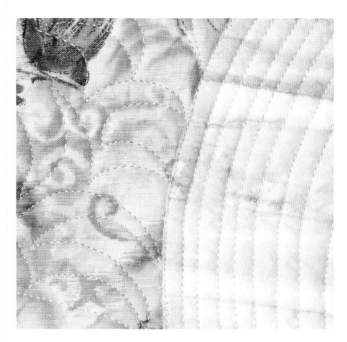

Raw edge seam on background sky piece

Captivating Coneflower, 17" x 22", © 2005

Dragonfly Embellishment

Sometimes you may want certain design elements to stand
out from the rest. One of the ways to do this is to create
a separate appliqué using fusible web. The image of this
dragonfly was applied with a fusible web and stitched with
specialty threads. The dragonfly fabrics are fused to the
background fabric.

Here is the dragonfly pattern you could try yourself.
Trace the different parts of the dragonfly onto the paper side
of the fusible web. For design parts that overlap, such as
the head and body or wings and body, add an extra ¼" to
accommodate the overlap. (*Note:* When working with fusible
web, your design will be reversed; it may be necessary to
reverse the original design before tracing.) When completed,
cut the traced sections out of the paper with a ⅛" surplus
all around.

Next, using the manufacturer's instructions, bond the
paper-backed web to the back sides of the chosen fabrics with
your iron. When the fusible is cool, cut the designs out directly
on the traced lines and peel the paper backing off. Lastly,
position fused fabrics onto your quilt top and iron the fused
fabrics in place according to the manufacturer's instructions.

Dragonfly embellishment adds a three-dimensional effect.

Pattern for dragonfly ready to be copied. (*Note:* Pattern is
reversed, as is typical for fusible-appliqué technique.)

Fabric variations from the subtle to the dramatic evoke the sense of being in a garden.

Pretty as a...
Picture in Yellow

Referring back to the original photograph of the prairie garden, I had many flowers to choose from for additional quilts. The yellow coneflower became another design subject.

The yellow coneflower is a prairie plant that I see frequently in the wild. It is less common in a cultivated garden, but when found, it often towers above the rest of the flowers with its yellow petals and brown centers reaching up for the sun.

Original photo

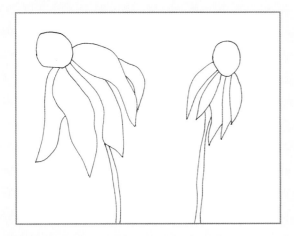

Line drawing

Quilter's Notes

Keeping It Simple

I know that tracing from a photograph has its limitations, so this is why I trace what I see, study the original photo, then tweak my line drawing.

When working with the flower as a subject, I might eliminate a petal or two and revise the curve of a petal line. I have the security of the exact line of the flower in front of me, but I also challenge my eye and my pencil to turn the tracing into a drawing *inspired* by the photograph.

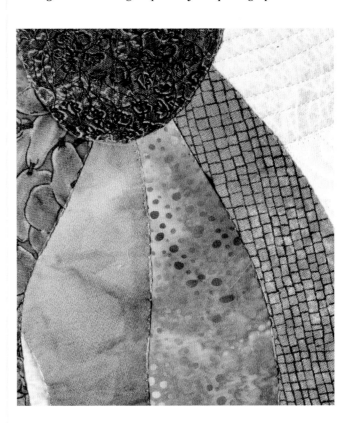

Focus on Fabrics

When your design lines are very simple, as they are in the yellow coneflower, let your fabrics take center stage. Fabrics with lots of visual texture add extra dimension and a sense of complexity to your finished project.

Pretty as a...Picture in Yellow, 14" x 19", © 2005

Coneflower Chorus

Continuing to ask myself the "What if?" question, I began to experiment with combining several successful tracings in a single quilt. I loved the single pink coneflower and decided to team it with several yellow "neighbors."

Line drawing

Quilter's Notes

Let There Be Light

For this quilt, I worked on combining multiple drawings in one design. My process? A window with daylight shining through became my light box. I simply taped the tracings to the window, and then moved my blank tracing paper around until I found a pleasing composition. Once satisfied, I traced my new design. Of course, if you have one, you can use a tabletop light box instead of a window.

Sometimes you may like to use a drawing or illustration program on the computer, or scan your tracings and work with them on the computer, to arrive at a pleasing composition.

Letting Ideas Blossom

Creating a pleasing composition takes time. Often, I create my line drawing, put it down for a day or so, and then go back and look at it with fresh eyes. We quilters have perfected the process of multi-tasking. I have numerous projects going on at any one time, and in various stages of progress. By working this way, I can design a new piece and let the design percolate, while at the same time have another piece ready for borders or quilting.

At the window, I create new designs on fresh copy paper using original tracings.

Coneflower Chorus, 19" x 25", © 2005

Hello Mr. Cardinal— It's Winter

Birds flutter about everywhere on our wooded property overlooking the lake. I look forward to the wrens' arrival each spring, and we see a cardinal family build a nest by our front door every May. Several cardinals flit about all year long, but they are particularly prominent against the white snow.

I enjoy watching these feathery creatures, but had not considered creating a cardinal quilt until a national quilt magazine approached me to do an article featuring my picture-image appliqué technique. I wanted to create a simple pattern that everyone would want to try...and the article was to appear in the December issue. The cardinal design was perfect for a winter theme.

Original photo

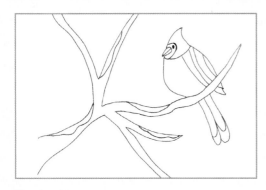

Line drawing

Quilter's Notes

Fabric "Speaks"

Fabric is such a great medium to work with. We can find a color, texture, or print to portray just about anything we want. As I traced the cardinal, I needed to keep the lines simple, and as I worked, I could already visualize fabrics that would speak "feathers" to me. (The non-quilters in the house know we truly have gone off the deep end when we describe that we hear fabric "speaking feathers."). I also found the perfect fabric for the snow on the branches that had just the right sparkle to it.

I could not stop at just one season with my cardinal quilt, and started asking "What if?" again.

Finding the right fabrics in our stash that "speak feathers" is a fun treasure hunt.

Fabric with a little bit of sparkle was perfect to depict snow on the branches.

Hello Mr. Cardinal—It's Winter, 22" x 17", © 2006

Hello Mr. Cardinal—It's Spring

21" x 17", © 2006

Of all the seasons, spring is my favorite—or at least the one I look forward to most. Winters are long in southwestern Wisconsin. When the first signs of spring finally arrive, we celebrate. As I look around outside, I am amazed at how many different greens I see: spring green, pine green, kelly green, sea green, and electric lime green. These visions of green motivate me to keep my stash stocked with a broad spectrum of green fabrics for the landscapes in my quilts.

Quilter's Notes

Textured Yarn

Here is yet another use for textured yarn. Couching yarn on the edge between the inside of the quilt and the border is an alternative to using a small traditional inner border. Pretty yarn can add just the right color and texture.

Use of couched yarn along the border of *Hello Mr. Cardinal—It's Spring* gives added textural interest.

Hello Mr. Cardinal—It's Summer

23" x 17", © 2007

I look out my windows and find the colors of summer so inspiring. I begin digging through my fabric stash and find many choices to interpret the colors of the season. It's great fun to see how those chosen fabrics look when the quilt is completed.

Quilter's Notes

Choosing Background Fabric

I refer many times to mottled and muckled fabrics and to using large-scale prints in quilts. In each cardinal quilt, I used four different fabrics for the background. Changing the placement of the fabrics and using them in several different areas of the quilt help tie the design together. The eye flows across the surface, connecting the repeated fabrics and colors to unify the overall design.

Samples of the background fabrics used in the cardinal quilts. It's a lot of fun to stretch yourself to find fabrics with unique visual appeal.

85

Climb Every Mountain

Deciding what quilt to begin next is always a challenge. We dream up so many great ideas, it is often difficult to narrow down our choices. A personal goal has been to create a body of work that is uniquely my own. I continually sort through family photos to determine which picture would work as the next "best" project. In addition, I am a member of several different art quilt groups, and we are always challenging each other to create pieces for future exhibits.

If I come across a challenge that allows me to create a piece for the event, and at the same time continue working on my picture quilts, I pursue it.

The ideal circumstances came together when I came across this photo of my husband, Tom. The photograph had been taken by his climbing partner when the two were climbing Mt. Shasta in Northern California. The action depicted in the photo offered great visual excitement as Tom hangs from the cliff's edge, and the unique perspective contributed to the visual interest.

The call for entries arrived from the Milwaukee Art Quilters in April 2005, and the theme was "Name that Tune." I spent several weeks working with the photograph, trying to determine what my "tune" would be. The assignment was to tell a visual story without words. Finally, the song "Climb Every Mountain" came to me, and I was off and running.

Quilter's Notes

Portraying Family Members

There are inherent challenges in creating quilts that depict family members. As artists, we have a vision of what we are trying to accomplish. Often, when we are working on the piece, we lose our direction or our confidence, so we seek feedback from others—sometimes from the family member who is also the subject of our work.

While working on *Climb Every Mountain*, I had the piece completely glue-appliquéd and decided to get Tom's opinion.

After viewing the project for a few minutes, he said, "I remember the rocks of the cliff a different color. They were not brown." Then he mentioned that he always wanted a handlebar mustache and perhaps I could change the more ordinary mustache he had in the original photo. He also noted that the climbing goggles he was wearing were a generic variety, and suggested I might change the design to something fancier so they would "look cooler."

I chuckle when I remember that exchange, but it demonstrates how powerful the observations of others can be. We need to be prepared to handle those opinions, and decide how we will respond. In the end, I kept the cliffs the way I visualized them and gave Tom his wonderful tried-and-true mustache and climbing goggles.

Line drawing

Original photo

Climb Every Mountain, 36" x 57", © 2004

Using Simple Lines to Create Stories

The Milwaukee Art Quilters' "Name that Tune" challenge had several parameters. First, the size of the piece had to be within an inch of 36" x 56"—very long and narrow. It had to include some kind of musical note and a three-dimensional embellishment.

I began the process of creating a line drawing of the photograph. Initially, I thought I would capture the various light sources and shadows. When I completed that drawing, I realized it looked too complicated. I tried again and was much happier with making simple tracings of the clothing, and sketching in only a few background lines.

My goal was to tell a visual story in keeping with the challenge, so I sketched in the stream and rainbow, taking the original design beyond its initial photographic boundaries.

Now, all I had to do was add a musical note, so I incorporated fabric with musical notes on the bottom of Tom's boot.

Texturizing the Cliff

The more I work with color values, the more freedom I feel when I go to choose fabrics. My interpretation of the cliff resulted in my use of medium-value browns. But within that collection of browns was a wonderful variety of prints and textures. For example, I included fabric with peacock feathers as well as a bit of cotton velveteen, which added tremendous visual depth and texture.

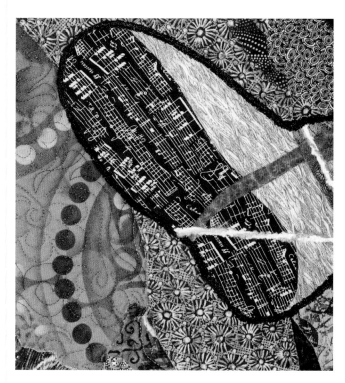

A musical note was added to the bottom of Tom's boot.

Finding fabrics in our stash that "speak feathers" helped me put this quilt theme together.

A small piece of striped fabric fused to the inner portion of the quilt creates a unique inner border.

Finishing with Harmonic Borders

As a quilt nears completion, I decide how I want to frame and finish the project. This is the point when I challenge myself to try something different, although I do have several techniques that I repeat on occasion. Some of these techniques are not mine exclusively, but they are the most effective for showcasing my pieces.

One finish I love is to have the inner design of the quilt flow into the border. In *Climb Every Mountain*, I achieved this by adding a narrow strip of striped fabric a few inches in from the outer edges of the quilt. After fusing, I machine stitched this small inner border with a programmed blanket stitch. Including stripes, plaids, and other geometric prints in your stash will offer you numerous unique choices for inner borders and bindings.

Often, too, I change the value of the design as it continues to the edge of the quilt to emphasize the border. If the inner area of the picture design is done in lighter values, I go to darker values as I approach the edges—and vice versa.

Carrying on with the technique of change in value, I like to do my randomly pieced borders in darker values. The darker value of the border really sets off the inner design effectively.

Another great finishing method is to border some of your pieces asymmetrically by placing borders on two sides of the quilt rather than on all four.

In the end, just remember to enjoy experimenting with a few different techniques before you make your final decision.

Climbing Rope

The couched yarn used for the climbing rope was my three-dimensional embellishment. I simply twisted several strands together and couched in place.

Multiple strands of yarn were twisted together and couched to create a textured climbing rope.

Changing the Details

In detailed areas of the face, I combine fusible web with picture-image appliqué. To change from the ordinary mustache to a fancy handlebar mustache, I took the original line drawing and, with tracing paper, made the changes to the mustache just as I changed the little girl's hairline to a little boy's.

Detail of original photograph

The face details were created with a little fusible web and some thread embellishing. This is what Tom would look like with a fancy handlebar mustache.

George the Entomologist— Catches the Quilting Bug

Portraying my dad, George Butler, at age 77 proudly displaying his first pieced quilt blocks makes me laugh with pure delight. After a lifetime career in entomology—a field that is up close and personal with insects—there is cause to celebrate George finding yet another creative passion: quilting.

This photograph of my dad was taken when he was visiting us from Arizona one fall. He had obtained numerous boxes of fabric strips from the homestead of his new wife's mother. Throughout Dad's entomology career, he had used the sewing machine to make bug nets, so when it came time to sew the strips, he already knew what to do. During the visit, he showed us the Log Cabin blocks he had started cranking out.

This project was an early attempt at the picture-image appliqué technique. I completed the line drawing of George, but then didn't know where to go next.

Quilter's Notes

Going Buggy

After much brainstorming, I decided on a lively background depicting the outdoors with insects all around. My collection of bug fabrics came in handy as I used them on the back of his quilt as well. The fun comes in being able to personalize the piece by weaving bits and pieces of my father's interests and personality into the quilt.

I knew my collection of bug fabrics would come in handy at some point. I used a few for the back of Dad's quilt.

Original photo

Line drawing

George the Entomologist—Catches the Quilting Bug, **47" x 48"**, © 2001

A Lifelike Butterfly

I found a wonderful large-scale print of butterflies and beetles, which I used to capture the entomologist theme. Some of the butterflies are fused directly onto the quilt top and others are created so that they seem to pop off the quilt.

To create my three-dimensional butterfly, I cut the butterfly print out of the fabric with an extra ¼" all around. Bonding fusible web to the back of the butterfly fabric, I then bonded that section to another piece of fabric with wrong sides together. Using a small zigzag stitch and black thread, I stitched around the outer edge of the butterfly. Then, I cut out the butterfly close to the edge of the zigzag stitch and zigzagged around the edge a second time.

To attach my butterfly, I stitched the project top around the abdomen of the butterfly, using monofilament thread in the top and bobbin. The extra support of the fusible web and two layers of fabric help the wings pop from the quilt top. This method can be used for large scale flowers, seashells or any other ideas that might come to you.

Quilt Block Replicas

My next brainstorm was to create Log Cabin blocks for the quilt using some of the fabrics my dad used in his quilt. When I called to ask him for some of the fabric strips, he said he had used them all to create three lap quilts, and the quilts had already been given away.

Finally, I found fabrics in my stash that resembled the vintage fabrics in the original blocks. It was fun to attach the unfinished quilt blocks directly to the finished quilt.

The Story Continues

George truly caught the quilting bug and continues to quilt with great gusto. He makes small lap quilts for local children's charities, using juvenile fabrics to make large medallion centers and adding many brightly colored borders. He machine quilts them in the ditch and completes at least two a week.

The quilt, *George the Entomologist—Catches the Quilting Bug,* has traveled to many quilt shows around the country, and George has served as a white glove volunteer standing next to his quilt. He is quite the hit among the attendees.

Using a large-scale print makes a great dimensional butterfly.

George pictured here with his quilt.

The unfinished pieced quilt blocks are added to the finished quilt top to create a three-dimensional look.

Behold the Beauty and Believe

It doesn't take much for me to get really excited about any project, but there are some pieces where the serendipitous connections of numerous special experiences merge in an almost magical way. This is what happened with *Behold the Beauty and Believe*.

The first experience occurred in 1998, when my husband and I accompanied my brother on one of his many mission trips to Mexico. While there, I took a photograph of a special vesper spot on the hill above Tlancualpican, Pueblo, Mexico. This photo remained in my file box for some time.

In the spring of 2005, my daughter Emily was confirmed at church. I wanted to commemorate this special event and remembered the photo of the vesper site. As I began to create the design and sort through my fabric stash I stumbled upon some hand-painted fabrics Emily had painted herself several years before. One of the pieces was perfect for the sky at sunset. It was as though it had been commissioned for the piece.

Original photo

Quilter's Notes

Outline Appliqué

I knew that the tree silhouettes would be tricky to create with my picture-image appliqué process, so I used an outline appliqué technique when applying the tree trunks to the quilt. The following paragraphs will illuminate this unique approach.

Once you have completed your quilt top background and it is fused to the fusible stabilizer, take your initial line drawing and trace the outline of the section you want to replicate the outline appliqué onto copy paper or newsprint. Choose the fabric for your outline appliqué and cut out a piece about 1" larger than the design. Lay the outline appliqué fabric on the quilt top in the place where you want the design, then pin the copy paper outline in place on top.

With a thread that blends with your outline appliqué fabric, machine stitch with a tiny stitch length following all around the traced lines on the copy paper. The stitches should perforate the copy paper. When finished, tear the paper away. Next, with appliqué scissors or other sharp scissors, cut away the excess fabric close to the *outside* of the stitching lines. What is left is the outline appliqué silhouette design.

To finish the process, I use a thread to enhance the outline appliqué fabric and stitch around each of the raw-edge seams with a free-motion scribble stitch. This will anchor everything in place and at the same time add some extra texture.

Line drawing

Behold the Beauty and Believe, **22" x 33",** © 2005

Remembering... in the Spring

My mother, Verna Mae Stroh Butler, was a strong, gentle, and quiet woman who was 75 years young when she died. She was born in Batavia, New York April 22, 1920 and died in Tempe, Arizona May 3, 1995, where she had lived for 46 years.

Our photo album is full of photographs of her in the education department of the Phoenix Zoo, at her grandchildren's birthday parties, and working in her prairie garden in Wisconsin. For several years, I contemplated creating a quilt featuring her. The photograph I kept returning to included my mom and my sons, Greg and Christopher, at Greg's sixth birthday party. It was a daunting project to tackle the three images, so I kept putting the photo away.

Finally, I decided to create the piece featuring just Verna Mae. After several attempts, I completed a line drawing that pleased me.

Original photo

Quilter's Notes

The Thumbnail

Again, numerous design challenges loomed ahead and the cold feet returned. I decided to create a "thumbnail" of mom's profile, figuring that working in a small format would be less daunting. Also, by working in the small format, I could work through the design challenges without feeling like I was working on my final masterpiece.

To create the thumbnail pattern, I enlarged the original drawing 210 percent. Using my pencil and some liquid correction fluid, I reworked the original line drawing some more, refining the facial features. Next, I made a freezer paper tracing of the thumbnail master image map, cut the fabrics out, and glue-appliquéd them together using the picture-image appliqué raw-edge method. The thumbnail assembled relatively quickly and I could get a sense of how my design and the fabric selections were working.

In the thumbnail size format I was able to study the original photograph, refer to the book, "Drawing from the Right Side of the Brain," and focus on her eyes, profile, and other facial features. Knowing the size of the final quilt would make mom's facial features very prominent, I critiqued my drawing carefully to make sure everything was in proportion.

Line drawing

Remembering...in the Spring, 45" x 41", © 2004

I refined Verna Mae's facial features after enlarging the original drawing 210 percent.

This thumbnail of Verna Mae is a smaller version created in fabric to test my design.

Daffodils Mean It's Spring

The last embellishments for this quilt were the fused daffodils. The flowers were cut from fused fabric, bonded to the border after the quilt top had been backed with fusible stabilizer, and then thread embellished before the quilt was layered with backing and batting. The daffodils were the final touch to emphasize the theme of spring. The quilt was completed in time to appear in the competition "Celebrate Spring."

Fused and embellished daffodil leaves and butterfly appear in the random-pieced border. Note the splash offered by the green-striped tiny tuck.

After testing the thumbnail, the final detailed version of my mother's image is shown here.

The Bear and the Boy— I Spy the Disappearing Bear's Paw

My first visit to the Museum of the American Quilter's Society in Paducah, Kentucky, was intoxicating. I spent hours enjoying the museum displays, including the "Storm at Sea" exhibit, which was the "New Quilts from an Old Favorite" competition for that year. The experience of viewing such amazing quilts, and seeing how the finalists had interpreted their designs, motivated me to create a quilt for the Bear's Paw competition the following year.

My initial design was inspired by my then-12-year-old son, Christopher, and his stuffed bear. I imagined the bear nearly full size. The image of the boy and the bear sitting next to each other, surrounded by traditionally pieced Bear's Paw blocks, came to me in the middle of the night.

Since I was not confident in my drawing skills, I took a photograph of Christopher posing as though he had his arm around the big bear. That photo was the start of the design. After sketching the outline from the photograph, I began to fill in the rest of the scene.

The story of the quilt emerged slowly. The bear is crying because his habitat is being destroyed. The boy represents future generations and the hope that—with compassion—young people can help stop the destruction of our natural environment.

Original photo

Quilter's Notes
Colors in Motion

Here's how I used the color wheel to plan and execute *The Bear and the Boy*. I started with my original sketch of the quilt and the fabric from my stash that I wanted to use for the body of the bear. I knew I would use a lot of earth tones and greens. The bear fabric had shades of burnt red and orange as well as browns and black. I picked up the color wheel, looked at green and orange, and then saw that if I chose purple as a third color, my color combination would be a triad. These became the main colors for my quilt.

I used various greens to represent the forested areas, browns and oranges for earth tones, and purples for the mountains. To confirm my color choices, I used colored pencils to shade in my sketch to see how they would work together. This step helped me see potential problem areas where I would need to use a darker value in one spot or a lighter value in another.

Once I knew the primary colors I wanted to focus on, I began pulling fabric from my stash that fell into those color groups. I needed to consider the value of the colors—light, medium, and dark. The value of the fabric is key to creating a dynamic design. The greater the difference in the value of your fabrics, the greater the contrast.

Line drawing

The Bear and the Boy—I Spy the Disappearing Bear's Paw, 73½" x 73½", © 2000

Color pencil rendering for the quilt

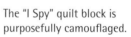

The "I Spy" quilt block is purposefully camouflaged.

Just for fun, here's an "I Spy" bear paw flower.

"Pawsing" for Thought

As I worked on the quilt, another inspiration came to me. I added an "I Spy" component to the design by hiding twenty-two full and partial Bear's Paw blocks within the body of the quilt (excluding the border). This humorous idea turned into a very popular aspect of the quilt.

As I added these new blocks, my challenge was to camouflage them rather than to create contrast. I chose fabrics of similar value for the Bear's Paws so they would be difficult to find in the quilt. When it came time to photograph the quilt for the jurying process, I needed to enhance many of these camouflaged blocks so the judges could see and appreciate the "I Spy" aspect of the quilt. To enhance the blocks, I couched yarns around them for emphasis.

Beyond Photographs

Don't wait for the perfect photograph. A future quilt can be designed using a photo-inspired drawing. Parts or all of a photo can be coupled with original sketches to complete the quilt.

Storytelling

As quilt artists, we are able to tell stories through our quilts—stories that can make a statement and provide insight into our thought process for the viewer.

The bears (and their paws) continue to disappear as our forest and other natural lands are destroyed by the clear-cutting of trees, construction of new roads, and increasing density of suburban populations. Cities, with their noise and pollution, appear on nearly every horizon. We can only hope that, with compassion and caring, the future generation can stop this destruction and save our bears and their paws.

This quilt was chosen as one of seventeen finalists in the American Quilter's Society's "Bear's Paw: New Quilts from an Old Favorite" contest years ago. It appears in their publication of the same name, was displayed in their museum for three months, and then toured for two years to different venues around the country.

The "I Spy" blocks on the body of the bear are enhanced for the camera's eye with couched yarn.

CHAPTER SIX

Quilt Gallery

This picture gallery essentially brings my work as an artist into the comfort of your own home—your own personal exhibition.

Up to now, you have been hard at work, learning my picture-image appliqué process, building up your tools and supplies, and absorbing the step-by-step process. Now it's time to step into my gallery, where I am delighted to share some more of my finished quilts.

The joy of these quilts is that each one is full of memories; just like a photo album, I never tire of gazing upon them and remembering the person or event that inspired them. Each one represents a specific challenge, requiring me to create a new skill or technique to solve it.

In short, each quilt was a special journey. When I view the quilts, they all bring a smile to my face as I reminisce about those journeys.

As I share my work with you, I hope you experience the pleasure and excitement of preserving memories with photo album quilts. Enjoy my stories and may you, too, be inspired.

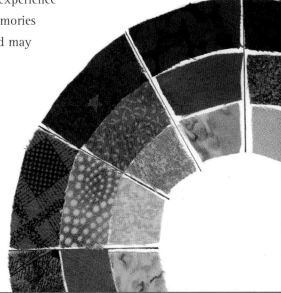

Be Gentle, the Future is Fragile

Themes for quilt contests lure me in. For this one, the 2000 Millennium Quilt Contest, there were five different categories. The one I was most intrigued by was "Wishes for the World." The judges asked for a 200-word artist statement to accompany the quilt, and here is part of what I wrote:

"Monarchs, manatees, monkeys, meadowlarks, mongoose, mankind—all share a tenuous future. My heart and soul wishes that we cultivate greater compassion for our natural world so that our children grow into benevolent caretakers of its future.

All living things exhibit wondrous life cycles. I hope each of us seeks opportunities with our children to study, explore, and appreciate these wonders. Only when we experience first-hand the sprouting of seeds, the hatching of chicks, or the transformations in a butterfly's lifecycle can we really begin to grasp the mysteries of our surroundings.

With the help of their grandpa, Emily, 2, and Christopher, 4, reared this monarch from an egg found on the milkweed. They saw an egg hatch, a caterpillar grow, a chrysalis form, and a butterfly emerge. Then with a gentle kiss, they let it go so it could migrate back to Mexico.

Techniques include curved machine piecing, some fusing, three-dimensional hand and machine appliqué, and machine quilting."

This continues to be a favorite quilt of mine. It features many early attempts at different quilting techniques and I learned much as a novice portraying the human form.

Growing up with my entomologist father has given me a special appreciation for all living creatures. Passing on that reverence and appreciation of nature to my children has always been one of my goals.

Creating this quilt and its artist statement truly came directly from the heart.

Original photo

Detail of quilt

Be Gentle, the Future is Fragile, **59½" x 53½",** © 2000

Together We Can

It was the last day of school and the third graders were in the midst of their field day at Monroe School in Hinsdale, Illinois. The image of all of these kids carrying the huge earth ball across the field was powerful. What a find when I dug this image out of the photo album. My son, Greg, is the blonde in the blue shirt.

On the playground the third graders race across the field carrying a huge earth ball. The group of eight children must work together with their combined strength and teamwork to keep the earth ball from toppling to the ground.

We can only hope that as our children grow and pursue positions of leadership, they will remember these simple moments on the playground and carry this spirit of teamwork and cooperation into the future, to strive towards peace and to help preserve the earth and all its inhabitants.

The background of the quilt is constructed of 2" squares and the earth of 1" squares. The quilt is machine appliquéd and machine quilted.

Detail of quilt

Original photo

Together We Can, 43" x 56½", © 2003

The World Is Yours

When my brother turned 40, I wanted to commemorate that milestone with a quilt. Larry has done mission work in Mexico since high school. He is also an accomplished photographer, having taken many wonderful photographs of the Mexican people he has worked with.

The quilt began with a photograph he had taken of a Mexican child holding a balloon with an image of the world on it. The rest of the design includes the bright colors of the Mexican marketplace and Seminole piecing in the borders. The paper-pieced people holding hands were perfect for an inner border. Along the bottom of the quilt are individual blocks created by family members with special messages to this very special brother, son, husband, and father.

The quilt includes paper piecing, machine and hand appliqué, hand embroidery, machine piecing, and machine quilting.

Original photo

Detail of quilt

The World Is Yours, **48" x 66",** © 1996

Solitude

"The best and the most beautiful things in the world cannot be seen or even touched. They must be felt with the heart." —Helen Keller

One Christmas, our family traveled to California. The trip began in San Francisco and ended in Santa Barbara for a visit with some cousins. Along the way there were wonderful sights to see. Wandering the beaches, exploring the tide pools, and swimming in the ocean were all part of our vacation.

This cloudy, rainy day was captured on film as my son, Greg, looked for starfish at Monterey Bay. The misty ocean's edge is a quiet place for reflection and wonder. At age 17 and six months from high school graduation, he appears pensive and I wondered what thoughts were flowing through his mind.

I captured this quiet moment on a quilt that is machine appliquéd and machine quilted.

Original photo

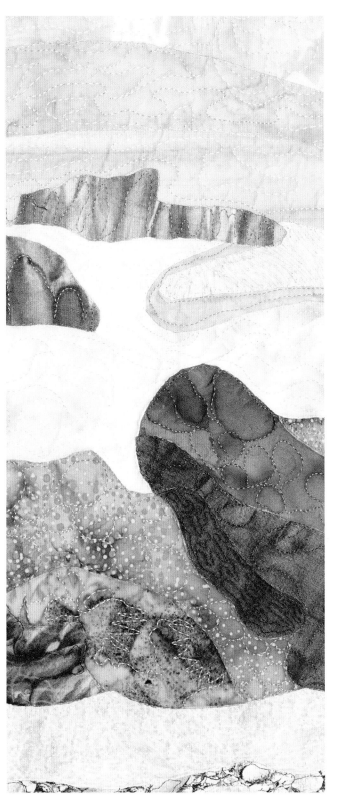

Detail of quilt

Solitude, **30" x 37½",** © 2004

W.B.B.—
Wendella B. Butterfly

When I look at what I created in this quilt, I know that I have really slipped off the edge.

This quilt was designed for the Milwaukee Art Quilters Challenge, "Self Portrait of the Artist as an Animal." It had to be approximately 40" x 50", hang vertically, have a frame like an old family portrait, have a nameplate in the bottom frame, and include some kind of embellishment.

Of all the quilts completed, mine was the only one that included the human form. When this group of quilts was displayed at the American Quilters Society show in Nashville, Tennessee, the show goers really had an entertaining time viewing the quilts and reading the individual artist statements. I was also pleased that my exhibit received third place in the Ultimate Guild Challenge that year.

Here is my quilt's story:

"Creeping caterpillars! How did this quilt artist get so buggy? WBB grew up with a father who is an entomologist (a bug guy). Combine that influence with the challenge to create a self-portrait of the artist as an animal and here's what happens.

Creeping caterpillars form chrysalis earrings, and finally the lovely monarch W.B. Butterfly emerges, ready to explore and experiment with the 'what ifs' of her art. The creative spirit flutters in the breeze and the directions for her flight are limitless."

The quilt was machine appliquéd and machine quilted, using bobbin drawing and three-dimensional embellishment.

Original photo

Detail of quilt

W.B.B.—Wendella B. Butterfly, 40¼" x 50½", © 2005

I Am

In Chapter 3 (see Repetition as a Design Element, page 41), I revealed my struggle to capture my son's mohawk hairstyle in a quilt—here's how it ended.

After much playing, I decided to create a small quilt of the teenager with the mohawk and see where it would lead. The original image was inspired by a photograph taken of my son, Christopher, in 2003, who was 15 at the time and sporting a mohawk hairstyle. The quilt was completed just in time for his birthday, so it became a gift.

Christopher is a man of few words, so when he opened up the box, all I heard as a response was a grunt. I will just have to imagine for myself what his true thoughts were.

For Christopher Berns
Happy 16th birthday!
"It is a curious and inescapable fact about our lives...That we cannot live without a cause, without some object of devotion, some center of worth, something on which we rely for our meaning."
—H. Richard Niebuhr
Love, Mom

The fabric collage technique for *I Am* was created using a water-soluble stabilizer. I created my own fabric using snippings of different colors, stitching them together between layers of water-soluble stabilizer. The picture image appliqué templates were cut out of the collaged fabric to create the image.

The quilt was machine appliquéd, embellished, and machine quilted.

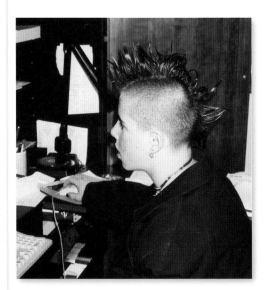

Original photo

Detail of quilt

I Am, 15" x 17", © 2004

Mountain Dream

When visiting beautiful places, the scenery is so amazing one often cannot capture it in a single photograph. The inspiration for a quilt sometimes can be a mix of many views and memories of a place. My mind blends these images into an interpretive design.

Good friends who love the mountains of the West commissioned me to create this quilt for their 24th wedding anniversary. I asked them what season of the year they envisioned and they chose summer.

The quilt was machine appliquéd and machine quilted.

To my good friends:
"Never lose the opportunity of seeing anything that is beautiful, For beauty is God's handwriting—a wayside sacrament. Welcome it in every fair face, in every fair sky, in every flower, and thank God for it as a cup of blessing."
—Ralph Waldo Emerson

Original photo #2

Detail of quilt

Original photo #1

Mountain Dream, **68" x 46"**, © 2005

Pure Joy...Imagine That!

As I sit at my computer and look at the images flooding the picture file, I am amused by all the silly photos taken by my teenage daughter and her friends. There is no censorship on the fun and delight that is captured in these images. How refreshing that is.

It was one of these images I thought of immediately when presented with the next challenge, "Master Pieces: Imagine That." The 5th Annual Husqvarna Viking Contest was at hand and I was eager to participate.

Designing this quilt flowed so smoothly that I was stunned at how all the pieces fell into place. Technical challenges arose, however, as I attached borders, evaluated value, and calculated how to arrive at a finished piece of exactly 51" square.

In brief, this was my quilt's story:

"Ahhh, to frolic with jubilant mirth and delight for no other reason than just for the pure pleasure of it. Imagine that!

It is time to rediscover what it is like to be young again. As we continue to age, let's bottle up that energy and spirit we experience from our children and make it our own."

What an honor it was to be told my quilt was chosen as one of the 50 finalists. An image of my quilt appears with the other finalists in a book, "MasterPieces—Imagine That!" and the quilt itself tours for two years in the United States, Europe, and Australia. It is sad to have the piece gone from my possession for so long, but exciting for it to be seen by so many people.

The quilt includes fusing, bobbin drawing, embellishing, machine appliqué, and machine quilting.

Original photo #1

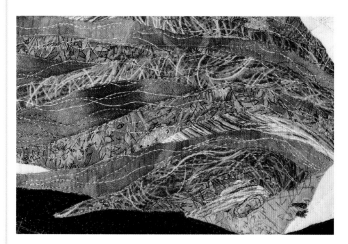

Detail of quilt

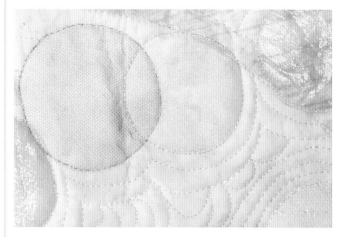

Detail of quilt

Pure Joy...Imagine That! 51" x 51", © 2006

About the Author

Wendy Butler Berns

Since 1993, Wendy Butler Berns has been capturing the world in quilts. Her quilt designs move beyond the realm of stitched fabric pieces to unexpectedly vivid tapestries that tell impressionistic stories. Her quilting style fluctuates between traditional-with-a-twist and contemporary art, and she often uses nature and real-life settings in photographs as her inspiration. Each design evolves through Wendy's desire to depict the colorful yet changing world around her—whether it be a garden landscape, an endearing family member, or an artistic reminder of the sanctity of our natural surroundings.

Wendy's quilts tell stories of people, places, and journeys that have shaped her life. Finding a way to interpret the messages from these stories has given her the chance to create original, tangible, and textural images that she can share with others.

Fabric and sewing have been a part of Wendy's life for more than 45 years. Her passion for the art of quilting is readily contagious; it inspires others to challenge their own creative boundaries and keeps her students marveling at her enthusiastic play of color, original design, embellishment, and unabashed free-motion quilting technique.

Since 1997, Wendy has traveled the country teaching and lecturing at national quilt conventions, quilting guilds, and quilting retreats. Described as an "enthusiastic, encouraging, entertaining, and knowledgeable teacher," Wendy strives to share her extraordinary art with anyone who wishes to learn it. Far from hiding her "trade secrets," Wendy hopes that her techniques, gained from hours of trial and error, will take root around the world.

Wendy's work appears regularly in publications such as *American Quilter, Quilter's Newsletter Magazine, Quilting Arts Magazine, The Quilting Quarterly*, and *Love of Quilting*. Books featuring her work include *The Ultimate Log Cabin Quilt Book, The Bear's Paw: New Quilts from Old Favorites*, and *MasterPieces—Imagine That!* She has produced quilts for galleries and juried shows, and private collections across the country.

When not creating new quilted art pieces, traveling, and preparing for workshops, Wendy enjoys her involvement with several art quilt groups and her local arts alliance, as well as gardening, running, and cycling the back roads of Wisconsin.

Wendy lives in Lake Mills, Wisconsin with her husband, Tom. She also looks forward to time with her daughter, Emily, and two sons, Christopher and Greg.
www.wendybutlerberns.com

Acknowledgments

Warm hugs to my family, who have been my biggest captive cheering section and unsuspecting subjects as I have sought to find my voice in quilt making.

Cheers to my husband, Tom, my patient sounding board, quilt photographer, webmaster, computer guru, and consultant who has helped me with all the things I didn't want to do, because I just desire to be a quilt artist.

Special thanks to my longtime friends who have bolstered my confidence along the way.

Best regards to my mentors, students, and fellow teachers in the quilting world with whom I have shared my passion for quilting and who have fed my spirit with inspiration.

Thank you to my editor, Erika Kotite, for holding my hand and offering encouragement on this wild roller coaster ride. You have skillfully nudged my words into just the right places.

Applause to Zachary Williams for capturing the essence of my quilts on film.

Thank you to Cathy Risling for keeping us on track.

My gratitude to Karen Carter, Mickey DePre, Maggi McCormick Gordon, Denise Havlan, and Jan Janes for lending their support, advice, and expertise to me along the way.

Resources

"The New Drawing on the Right Side of the Brain"
by Betty Edwards
©1999 Putnam Publishing Group
ISBN13: 9780874774245
ISBN10: 0874774241

Décor Bond by Pellon
Fusible stabilizer, 42" wide, product #809
Pellon Consumer Products
www. pellonideas.com
www.shoppellon.com

Metric Equivalency Charts

mm-millimeters   cm-centimeters
inches to millimeters and centimeters

inches	mm	cm	inches	cm	inches	cm
1/8	3	0.3	9	22.9	30	76.2
1/4	6	0.6	10	25.4	31	78.7
1/2	13	1.3	12	30.5	33	83.8
5/8	16	1.6	13	33.0	34	86.4
3/4	19	1.9	14	35.6	35	88.9
7/8	22	2.2	15	38.1	36	91.4
1	25	2.5	16	40.6	37	94.0
1 1/4	32	3.2	17	43.2	38	96.5
1 1/2	38	3.8	18	45.7	39	99.1
1 3/4	44	4.4	19	48.3	40	101.6
2	51	5.1	20	50.8	41	104.1
2 1/2	64	6.4	21	53.3	42	106.7
3	76	7.6	22	55.9	43	109.2
3 1/2	89	8.9	23	58.4	44	111.8
4	102	10.2	24	61.0	45	114.3
4 1/2	114	11.4	25	63.5	46	116.8
5	127	12.7	26	66.0	47	119.4
6	152	15.2	27	68.6	48	121.9
7	178	17.8	28	71.1	49	124.5
8	203	20.3	29	73.7	50	127.0

yards to meters

yards	meters	yards	meters	yards	meters	yards	meters	yards	meters
1/8	0.11	2 1/8	1.94	4 1/8	3.77	6 1/8	5.60	8 1/8	7.43
1/4	0.23	2 1/4	2.06	4 1/4	3.89	6 1/4	5.72	8 1/4	7.54
3/8	0.34	2 3/8	2.17	4 3/8	4.00	6 3/8	5.83	8 3/8	7.66
1/2	0.46	2 1/2	2.29	4 1/2	4.11	6 1/2	5.94	8 1/2	7.77
5/8	0.57	2 5/8	2.40	4 5/8	4.23	6 5/8	6.06	8 5/8	7.89
3/4	0.69	2 3/4	2.51	4 3/4	4.34	6 3/4	6.17	8 3/4	8.00
7/8	0.80	2 7/8	2.63	4 7/8	4.46	6 7/8	6.29	8 7/8	8.12
1	0.91	3	2.74	5	4.57	7	6.40	9	8.23
1 1/8	1.03	3 1/8	2.86	5 1/8	4.69	7 1/8	6.52	9 1/8	8.34
1 1/4	1.14	3 1/4	2.97	5 1/4	4.80	7 1/4	6.63	9 1/4	8.46
1 3/8	1.26	3 3/8	3.09	5 3/8	4.91	7 3/8	6.74	9 3/8	8.57
1 1/2	1.37	3 1/2	3.20	5 1/2	5.03	7 1/2	6.86	9 1/2	8.69
1 5/8	1.49	3 5/8	3.31	5 5/8	5.14	7 5/8	6.97	9 5/8	8.80
1 3/4	1.60	3 3/4	3.43	5 3/4	5.26	7 3/4	7.09	9 3/4	8.92
1 7/8	1.71	3 7/8	3.54	5 7/8	5.37	7 7/8	7.20	9 7/8	9.03
2	1.83	4	3.66	6	5.49	8	7.32	10	9.14

Index